BUILDING RESILIENCY in Teens

A Trauma-Informed Workbook for Teens

Also from the Boys Town Press

Building Resiliency in Youth: A Trauma-Informed Guide for Working with Youth in Schools
Building Resiliency in Teens: A Trauma-Informed Activity Guide for Children
Teaching Social Skills to Youth, 3rd Ed.
Teaching Social Skills to Youth with Mental Health Disorders
Well-Managed Schools, 2nd Ed.
Tools for Teaching Social Skills in School
Everyone's Talking
Take Two: Skill-Building Skits You Have Time to Do!
13 & Counting: Be the Difference
13 & Counting: Does a Hamburger Really Have to Be Round?
13 & Counting: Rescue Me
GRIT & Bear It!
GRIT & Bear It! Activity Guide
Zest: Live It
Zest: Live It Activity Guide
Positive Alternatives to Suspension
Working with Aggressive Youth
No Room for Bullies
Safe and Healthy Secondary Schools
Common Sense Parenting®

For a free Boys Town Press catalog, call 1-800-282-6657
Visit our website at BoysTownPress.org

Boys Town National Hotline®
1-800-448-3000
A crisis, resource, and referral number for kids and parents
YourLifeYourVoice.org

BUILDING RESILIENCY in Teens

A Trauma-Informed Workbook for Teens

Kat McGrady, ED.D., LCPC, NCC

Boys Town, Nebraska

Building Resiliency in Teens: A Trauma-Informed Workbook for Teens
Published by Boys Town Press
Boys Town, NE 68010

Copyright © 2021 by Father Flanagan's Boys' Home

ISBN: 978-1-944882-80-8

All rights reserved. Though this resource is intended for individual use, permission is granted for the purchaser of this resource to reproduce pages 4-86 for individual or small group counseling only. No other part of this book may be reproduced or transmitted in any form or by any means, electronic or mechanical, including photocopying, recording, or by any information storage and retrieval system, without the written permission of Boys Town Press, except where permitted by law. For information, address Boys Town Press, 13603 Flanagan Blvd., Boys Town, NE 68010 or btpress@boystown.org.

 Boys Town Press is the publishing division of Boys Town, a national organization serving children and families.

10 9 8 7 6 5 4 3 2

TABLE OF CONTENTS

Teen Workbook: What's in It for You?	1

PROCESSING FEELINGS, EMOTIONS, BEHAVIORS, AND ACTIONS

The Balancing Act	4
Bottled Emotions	7
Totem Pole Tales	9
iRobot	14
This Just In!	17
To Whom it May Concern	21
Dear, Me	23
SING Like a Rockstar	28
Choose Your Own Adventure	31
Reflection Pages	38

COPING, GROUNDING, AND CALMING

SPLAT!	44
Nourishing Nature	46
Swing, Sway, Oscillate, Pendulate	48
Strategy Sampling	50
Serenity Strings	53
Secret Silent Whisper Shout	54
We've Got the Beat	56
Bon Voyage!	58
Lighthouse Beacon Flexes and Senses	60
Reflection Pages	63

CONFIDENCE-BOOSTING, STRENGTH, AND RESILIENCE

Playlist Twist	70
Personal Bill of Rights	71
Kintsugi Bowl	73
My Personal Slogan	75
Catch of the Day	78
Back to the Future	82
My Refreshing Cycle Plans	84
Opting for Optimism	90
Reflection Pages	94

Instructions to Download Worksheets and Handouts

ACCESS:

https://www.boystownpress.org/book-downloads

ENTER:

Your first and last names

Email address

Code: 944882BRT808

Check yes to receive emails to ensure your email link is received

Teen Workbook: What's in It for You?

We all have a "thing." In fact, we usually have more than one "thing." Regardless of skill or talent, or how popular it is amongst our peers, we all have those "things" that both speak to us and that allow us to speak out when words just aren't enough. They pacify us when we are upset. They clear away mind clutter when we can't think straight. They give us that feeling of satisfaction and fulfillment, even if we are the only ones who get to experience the process and the outcome.

Our "thing" isn't necessarily something that we have mastered. We may not create art on the level of Rockwell or da Vinci but, maybe drawing squiggly lines or watching paint flow from our brush onto canvas gives us an unmatched sense of pleasure and comfort. We may not run like Usain Bolt or dance like Misty Copeland but, a 20-minute scenic mile or dancing in our living room may give us a quick spark of joyful energy like nothing else.

Our "thing" may perk up our senses (e.g., the sounds of your favorite playlists, the smells, tastes, and feeling of sipping a piping cup of coffee) or give us a voice that does not require speaking (e.g., creating your own music, exploring flavors, scents, and tastes through cooking).

This workbook allows for the exploration of those "things" that are uniquely yours. That may mean freshly discovering "things" that stimulate wellness and renewal within you, or it may mean revisiting and refining the "things" that already invigorate and encourage positive growth. The first section provides activities and ideas for self-reflection and processing. This will help you to better understand yourself, what drives you, what elicits feelings and emotions, and what lens through which you see the world. That understanding of self will lend itself to the next section, which nurtures exploration of those "things" that spark something within. This section provides foundational ideas that you can use as a springboard to find those "things" that are uniquely yours and that give you a sense of:

- balance and control,
- tranquility and safety,

- connection to self and to the world around you,
- empowerment and strength, and
- accomplishment.

The final section then brings everything together. It provides a means for you to use these personal discoveries to boost your ability to accept and cope with undesirable situations while continuously strengthening your resilience.

Each section is followed by "Reflection Pages." Reflection helps us to be more self-aware. It allows us to see where we are, where we want to go, how we will get there, and how we are doing along the way. It keeps us on track, highlights what is most important to us, allows us to be purposeful in our actions, and acts as a quick reminder of the things we forget.

For example, think of your favorite celebrity or person with an impressive skill. An actor, singer, athlete, carpenter, baker, veterinarian, anyone that comes to mind. To reach success in their field, that person had to build on their understanding and their natural capabilities. They may have already been good at their craft, but they had to reflect on their areas of growth, learn, and continuously reflect on what/how to improve. In fact, I would guess that they continue to practice reflection and unrelenting improvement well-beyond the moment they found success.

After you have completed each section, take some time to reflect on what you learned and what you can do with that new knowledge. The "Immediate Reflection Notes" page will provide you with a way to highlight meaningful discoveries and to plan next steps that are personalized to you.

The "Self Check-In Reflection Notes" page assists you in following up and modifying any steps as needed. Keep in mind that there is no "wrong answer" or "failure" when self-reflecting. Rather, self-reflection entails providing insights that are right *for you* and providing ways to modify steps in order to successfully reach goals.

As you complete the activities in this workbook, keep these considerations in mind:

- This workbook is yours and yours alone. You set the tone and you set the pace of completion.
- The "correct" answers or outcomes are those that make you feel satisfied.
- You can make the activities in this workbook whatever you choose to make them. If you feel that modifying some directions would meet your personal needs and increase the outcomes of some activities, feel free to do so.
- Try to be as open and honest with yourself as possible while completing these activities. That is the best way to maximize their benefits.
- Try to save this workbook upon completion. You will find it useful down the road when new situations arise and you want a quick "personal cheat sheet" for coping, or when you feel curious and want to look back at who you were while completing this workbook versus who you have become.

Processing Feelings, Emotions, Behaviors, and Actions

Emotional processing involves awareness of emotions, acceptance of and comfort with emotions, and the ability to work through emotions in a healing and nourishing way. Many consider emotional processing to be the first step in strengthening resiliency, as recognizing, understanding, and nonjudgmentally absorbing emotions allows us to choose the best options moving forward.

The following activities are intended to promote healthy emotional processing. They help to build a strong emotional foundation, which then allows for restorative coping and responsiveness as opposed to destructive repression or reaction. These activities are most beneficial when used in the initial stages of a resiliency plan. Emotional processing and reflection should then be a common theme and revisited often thereafter.

The Balancing Act

Think of your feelings as a seesaw.

One side is completely ideal. The dream life. You feel nothing but bliss and joy and extreme happiness.

The other side, however, is completely awful. It's that side that makes you feel nothing but sadness, fear, and anger.

Usually, we fall somewhere in the middle. We find that sweet spot that levels our seesaw out and keeps us balanced. We may have some stressors and experiences that leave us feeling a little "off," but for the most part, we are content, stable, and feeling "A-OK."

Sometimes though, we get caught up in one portion of our lives and completely neglect the rest. That leads us to lose our footing and tip the balance of our seesaw. When this happens, it can make us feel even worse. It can cause us to topple even further down that side of our seesaw.

That is why it is important we stay focused and mindful of our footing on the seesaw.

Purpose of Exercise:

- Reflect on the essential wellness points.
- Identify areas of strength and growth in each area of wellness.
- Determine an action plan for increasing overall well-being.

What You Will Need:

- *My Balancing Act* pages

Each square below represents a piece of your life.

Directions:

1. Within each square, draw a seesaw to show how balanced you feel in that particular area or your life.

2. If you feel unbalanced in a negative way, tilt your seesaw to the degree that you feel that negative unbalance towards the left.

   Example:

3. If you feel that things are better than normal, tilt your seesaw to the degree that you feel this towards the right.

   Example:

4. If you feel like you are "normal" or "just fine," keep your seesaw straight.

   Example:

5. On the left side of the square, write words that describe things that aren't going well or things you would like to work on in this area of your life.

6. On the right side of the square, write words that describe things that are going well and you enjoy in terms of this area of your life.

   Example:

PERSONAL GROWTH	
- Want to learn how to play guitar - Have not drawn in a long time - Haven't taken steps towards getting out more	- Learning how to bake - Started exercising - Signed up for a class to learn Spanish

My Balancing Act

PERSONAL GROWTH	RECREATION/FUN
SPIRITUALITY	FRIENDSHIPS
LOVE INTERESTS	FAMILY
SCHOOL	MENTAL HEALTH
PHYSICAL HEALTH	SELF-CARE/"ME TIME"

Bottled Emotions

Purpose of Exercise:

- Reflect on the negative effects that occur when we bottle up emotions or don't seek support when needed.
- Identify ways to share emotions safely.

What You Will Need:

- An empty 1-liter plastic bottle
- About a cup of hydrogen peroxide
- 4 tbsp warm water
- Dish soap
- One package of active dry yeast (found in the baking aisle of the grocery store)
- A large space to work in (a countertop or outside works well)

Directions:

1. Pour the hydrogen peroxide into the liter bottle.
2. Add a squirt or two of dish soap.
3. In a separate cup, stir together the warm water with a package of dry active yeast, allowing the yeast to dissolve in the water.
4. Pour the yeast into the liter bottle along with the hydrogen peroxide and the dish soap.
5. Wait a few moments.
6. Reflect on what you observed.
7. Consider this experiment in the following way:
    a. The bottle represents you. The other ingredients represent bottled up emotions, bad experiences, and other negatives that you may hold onto without seeking or accepting support.
    b. When you bottle up emotions and/or do not seek or accept help from others to resolve these emotions, they eventually spill out. Often in ways that leave a mess to clean up. This mess can be outbursts or actions that negatively impact your relationships with others, or that leave you feeling worse than before.

c. It is vital to not only seek out, but to accept support when you're experiencing negative emotions or events. It may seem scary, unnecessary, burdensome, or like a weak way out at first, but all of these ideas are untrue:
    i. It takes great courage and strength to ask for help or support when you need it.
    ii. It makes others feel good, knowing that you trust them and that you feel they are worthy of supporting you.
    iii. We all need support from time to time. We cannot go at this life alone and should not attempt to do so.

8. Now, think about how to ask for help in a way that you are comfortable with. Consider the following:
    a. Who are trusted adults and friends I can turn to (at home, in school, at work, in after-school activities, parents of friends, others)?
    b. What words can I use to express that I would like their help or that I need to share something with them?
    c. What can I do or say if they don't understand or respond in a way that comforts me and shows that I am being heard?

Totem Pole Tales

You may have learned about totem poles in class, at museums, in shows and books, or maybe you have even seen one in real life!

Totem poles inspire respect and a sense of kinship or connection in many Native American cultures. They are pillared monuments, usually carved out of wood, that represent events, heritage, or other items of significance to those who create them. Totem poles often are constructed of carved animals tiered together like a layer cake. Each animal, color, or shape usually holds a symbolic significance.

Totem poles tell stories. They are awe-inspiring and representative of something much deeper than what meets the eye.

What would your totem pole look like?

Let's take a moment to figure that out! Below are a few totem pole activities. These are meant to help you reflect, consider, sort, and create your story. They are:

- *Totem Pole Total Loves*
- *Totem Pole of Positivity*
- *Symbols of Self*
- *Totem Pole Possibilities*

Remember, these are your totem poles, your stories, and they can be whatever you choose to make them. Have fun and tell the stories you want to tell!

Purpose of Exercise:

- Reflect on values, goals, and self.
- Prioritize who/what is most important.

What You Will Need:

- *Totem Pole Total Loves* page
- *Totem Pole of Positivity* page
- *Symbols of Self* page
- *Totem Pole Possibilities* page

 The *Totem* activity pages are available for download so that you can revisit these pages and change them as you continue to write your story! See download instructions under the Table of Contents.

BUILDING RESILIENCY IN TEENS

Totem Pole Total Loves

DIRECTIONS: Consider the people in your life who you love and respect, and those who love and respect you. This could be family, friends, teachers, coaches… anyone. Label them in each totem shape below. Remember to put yourself on the top of the totem pole. After all, you are very important and should be chief in the love and respect department. You may also add more shapes and layers if you'd like.

A Trauma-Informed Workbook for Teens

Totem Pole of Positivity

DIRECTIONS: Take a moment to reflect on all the good that you bring to the world. Even on your worst days, you still have amazing skills and qualities that add a little bit more goodness and positivity to the world.

Even if the skill is something as small as knowing how to draw a perfect heart or knowing how to hammer in a nail. Even if the quality is something as seemingly small as being dependable or being sincere or being a good listener. All of these skills and qualities make you who you are and give you something that many others don't have.

In this totem, write the top skills and qualities that make you YOU. You may add more pillars and shapes to the totem pole, if you would like.

Symbols of Self

DIRECTIONS: Think about the elements that make up your unique story. These elements could be:

- Unique traits, qualities, and skills
- Emotions
- Memories and significant events
- Significant people in your life
- Your hopes and dreams
- The person you desire to become

In the space below, illustrate a totem pole that represents your story. Use colors, symbols, shapes, animals, and/or other representations to symbolize these important features of *you*. Remember, this is *your* story, *your* interpretation, and there is no wrong in what *you* choose to create.

Totem Pole Possibilities

DIRECTIONS: Reflecting back on your previous totem poles, consider how these tie into your aspirations for the future.

Who do you want to become? What kind of person would you like to be? Think about elements such as:

- Traits, qualities, and skills you want to strengthen
- People who you look up to or aspire to be like
- What career you would like to have
- Where you want to be and who you'd like to surround yourself with
- What would bring you joy every single day, even on bad days

In the space below, illustrate a totem pole that represents your future story. Use colors, symbols, shapes, animals, and/or other representations to symbolize the things that you aspire towards. Remember, this is your story, your interpretation, and there is no wrong in what you choose to create.

iRobot

The human mind and body are amazing things. We are almost like robots! Think about it….

A robot is controlled by an external force, like a remote control or something that provides information and gives it commands. That robot then computes what is being asked of it and reacts accordingly.

If you want to turn your phone on, for example, you press the "Power" button. What happens? It turns on! Maybe you want to search for the best local coffee shop. You pop into your Yelp app or just input the information you're looking for in your web browser and before you know it, the best latte spots are right at your fingertips!

Our minds and bodies kind of act in the same manner. We gather information from an external control (our environment, experiences, what is happening around us) and we use that information to activate our emotions and bodies to respond.

Just like our devices can glitch sometimes (miscompute data, get infected, etc.), our minds can glitch, too. We may misperceive data in our environment. That can impact how we feel, which then impacts how we react and respond.

Have you ever said "Hi" to a friend in the hallway, only to have them blow you off? Feels horrible, doesn't it? It makes your stomach drop. It makes your body go limp. It makes you wonder what you did to upset them. You respond by texting an angry and hurt "What did I do?" Then, you find out your friend had their earbuds in and didn't hear or see you. That is a mind glitch! You misperceived the data provided to you and it impacted your feelings and responses.

This happens more often when a personal trigger occurs. It may be someone raising their hand for a "high five," a loud noise, a facial expression, a word… there are a number of triggers that can send our minds back to a negative event that we experienced in the past, even if the present experience is nothing like what we had experienced before. These triggers impact our feelings and our responses in ways that may be disconnected to the present and in ways that are hurtful or unhealthy.

This is why it is important we recognize our triggers and how they impact our feelings and responses. If we recognize what triggers us, we can avoid that initial negative thought, which would then avoid a hurtful or unhealthy response. Mind glitch, averted!

Purpose of Exercise:

- Recognize triggers, and their physiological and their emotional impact.
- Identify the thoughts that accompany triggers.

What You Will Need:

- *iRobot* activity page

Directions:

1. Use the provided *iRobot* chart to identify your triggers. When they occur, jot them down.

2. Pay careful attention to your body in these moments. Write down what you are physically feeling in the moment that is triggering you. Sometimes, it helps to close your eyes and pretend like there is a spotlight on each part of your body. Place the spotlight on your head and focus on what you are feeling in that area only. Then, move the spotlight to your neck, shoulders, chest, etc.

3. Be mindful of your inner self-talk in the moment. Write down thoughts that your mind is telling you. In the next activity, we will learn how to challenge these thoughts, how to counter the triggers and thoughts, and how to respond in a positive and healthy way.

Example:

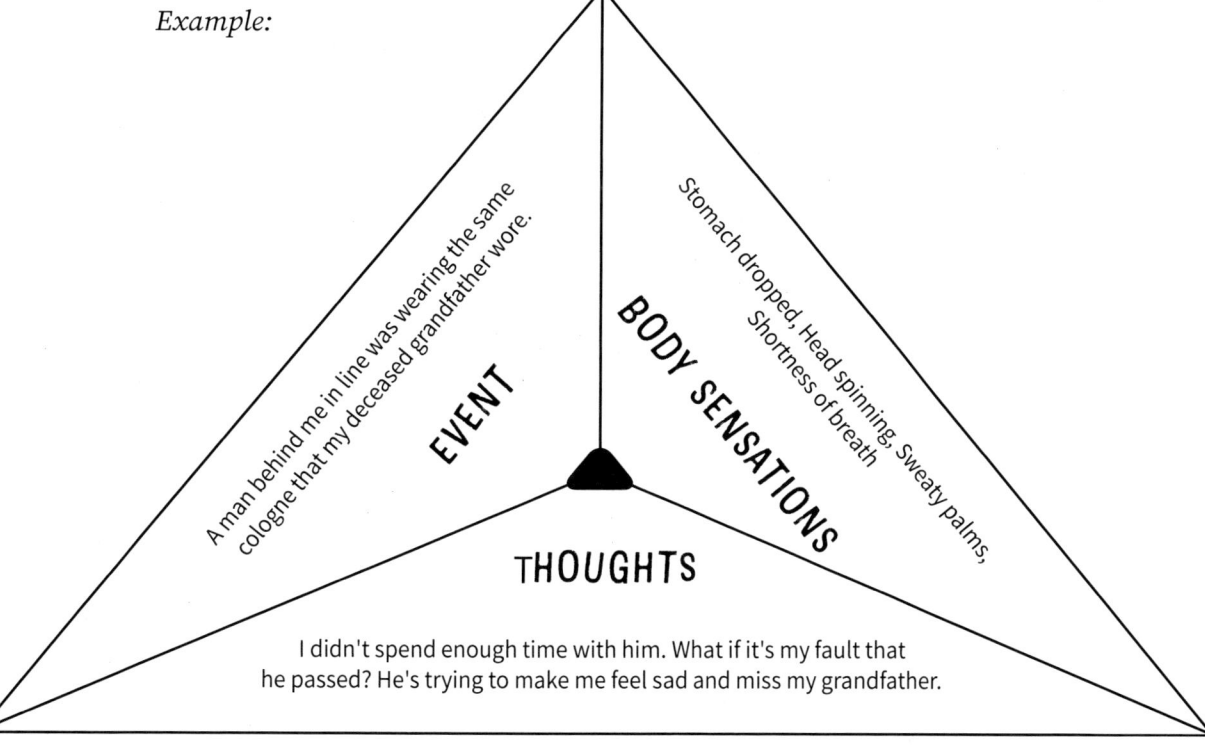

iRobot

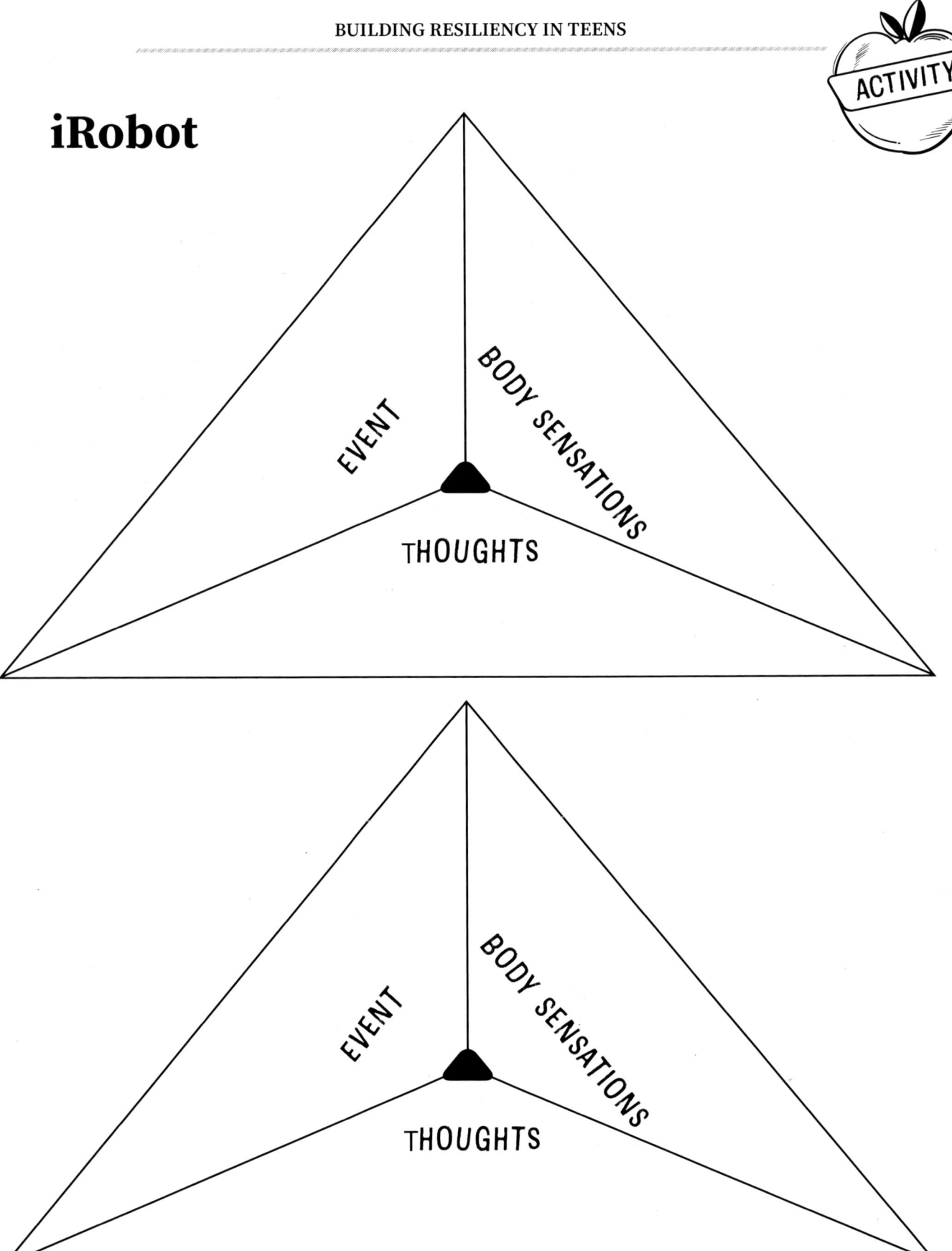

NOTE Additional *iRobot* charts are available for download. *See download instructions under the Table of Contents.*

This Just In!

Do you ever watch the news on TV? When something occurs, a reporter is sent out to the location of the occurrence. This could be something as scary as a tornado touching ground, or something as fun as a carnival coming to town. The job of reporters is to share what happened in a non-biased way. They explain what occurred. Oftentimes, they find bystanders (or people who witnessed the event) to share firsthand accounts, and to get a variety of vantage points of the happening so viewers can get a well-rounded sense and form their own opinions without being swayed one way or the other.

Sometimes, we can misinterpret events that occur in our own lives. We tell ourselves stories based on past experiences that impact our ability to see current events in a non-biased way. When we can only see the stories in our lives through our own vantage point, we don't get the full story.

In those moments when we feel upset or confused by current situations, it is helpful to step outside of our own thoughts and pretend like we stepped into the news. To look at what is happening to us through the eyes of a reporter and the eyes of bystanders.

Stepping out of our own biased thoughts and strengthening our ability to see events as others may see them is a powerful skill. It allows us to gain clarity, resilience, and maintain an overall healthy and realistic outlook on our life stories.

Purpose of Exercise:

- Recognize how to look at a situation from many angles.
- Understand how to find and take on the most positive viewpoint.

What You Will Need:

- *This Just In!* short answer pages and comic strip (optional)

Directions:

1. Consider a recent event that left you feeling distressed, neglected, angry, or any other undesirable emotion. Write the event here:

   _____
   _____
   _____
   _____

2. What did this event remind you of? Did you have similar feelings and/or a similar experience in your past? Write about it here:

   _____
   _____
   _____
   _____

3. Pretend you are a reporter. Step outside of your own thoughts and your understanding of what occurred. How would a reporter share what occurred? If you were an outsider looking in and just reporting what you observe, what would you say?

   _____
   _____
   _____
   _____

4. Now, pretend like you are a bystander. What is one way that person may explain this event? What is one way of looking at this experience?

   _____
   _____
   _____
   _____

5. In order to get multiple perspectives, pretend like you are yet another bystander who wants to chime in. What is yet another way of looking at this event?

_____

_____

_____

_____

6. Continue to play out the story as if hearing it from other people with varying vantage points. Try to give these bystander accounts a positive spin on what occurred.

7. Choose the account you feel is most helpful, healthy, and positive. Keep telling yourself this account of the event.

8. If you'd like, you may complete the provided *This Just In!* comic strip to tell the story of the news report. Illustrate the event, the reporter's observations, and the bystander accounts. You may want to add in speech bubbles, narrations, or anything that you see fit.

This Just In!

To Whom it May Concern

When applying for a job, you often need to provide a cover letter along with your application. A cover letter is sort of like the **snap shots** that you may have seen in this workbook or the guide. It is meant to spotlight your awesomeness to a potential boss. You may add details about your experiences, your skills and strengths, and what makes you the perfect person for the job.

Cover letters usually begin with something along the lines of *"To Whom it May Concern"* since you may not know the name of the person who will be reviewing your job application.

Today, you are going to write a *"To Whom it May Concern"* letter that highlights your experiences, your overall awesomeness, and how your experiences and awesomeness will help you to create the best life ever. The only difference is this letter won't be to highlight this good stuff to a potential boss. Instead, this letter will highlight this good stuff to a person or experience that may have caused you to have unwelcome thoughts or feelings. It is a way of giving yourself closure and letting that person or experience know the situation did not break you. Instead, it made you stronger and you will use what you gained from it to reach your goals.

Rather than sending this letter out, you will keep it for yourself. It will serve as a reminder of your resilience, your ability to overcome challenges, and of your overall awesomeness.

Purpose of Exercise:

- Gain a sense of closure in a negative experience.
- Express feelings to someone who has caused negative thoughts or harm.

What You Will Need:

- Paper and writing utensil

Directions:

1. Think of someone or something that you would like to share your thoughts with. This can be about someone or something, such as an unwelcome experience or event, that you feel has impacted you in an unfavorable way.
2. Write this person, experience, or event in a "To whom it may concern" letter.

3. In the first paragraph, express to them things that you otherwise feel you could not share. Provide snapshots and highlights that you need this person, experience, or event to know. Some ideas could include:
    a. How they/it made you feel
    b. Why they/it made you feel that way
    c. How their actions/it has impacted you since
4. In the next paragraph, express to them the things that helped you, or will help you, to overcome. Share important things, such as:
    a. Your traits, values, and strengths that will help you to move forward
    b. The qualities you possess that make you better than them/it
    c. The reasons why you deserve to move forward with happiness and positivity
    d. How you will use what you experienced to become stronger and to live the life you want to live
5. Read what you wrote and reflect on it. What are you feeling now that you have expressed what you need to express? What are you feeling now that you can see, on paper, what you felt and how you can/will move forward with happiness and positivity?
6. Keep the letter in a safe place. Revisit it whenever you need this reminder.

Dear, Me

We all have different experiences, good and bad. It is how we respond to those experiences that shape who we are and who we will become:

- If we see setbacks and challenges as things from which to learn, to overcome, and become a stronger person, then our outcomes will be positive and successful. However, if we see setbacks and challenges as reasons to give up, get angry, or become resentful, then our outcomes will most likely be unfulfilling and gloomy.
- If we see good fortune and luck as something deserved without work or care, then our outcomes may end up lacking. However, if we see good fortune and luck as things to be grateful for or things that resulted from hard work and determination, then our outcomes will be satisfying and fulfilling.

The way we see the world is essential in how we exist in it. If you believe in gratitude, optimism, and hard work in learning from your experiences, and in taking control of how you respond to whatever gets thrown your way, then you will reach your goals and lead a happier life.

In this activity, you will be writing, or sending voice-recorded messages, to your past and your future self. You will provide your past self with: (a) hopeful and optimistic outlooks on past experiences, (b) reassurance, and (c) care; and will provide your future self with: (a) advice, (b) inspiration, and (c) a way to see positive and/or purpose in all situations.

Purpose of Exercise:

- Reflect on how experiences have impacted me.
- Reassure and give advice to past self.
- Give a pep talk to future self.

What You Will Need:

- *Dear, Me* short answers
- *Dear Past Self* page
- *Dear Future Self* page

Directions:

1. Decide which platform you'd prefer: writing letters or using your phone to record audio letters.

2. Begin by writing/recording a letter to your past self. If it helps, pretend like this letter is meant to support a close friend or family member. Before you begin your "Dear Past Self" letter, take a moment to reflect on the following:

   a. Moments that left you feeling unhappy, unresolved, or that you feel shaped your outlook in a less-than-favorable way.

   _____
   _____
   _____

   b. People, places, items, or personal traits you feel helped you through these moments.

   _____
   _____

3. Now, begin your letter. Be sure to start by empathizing with your past self. Explain that you know what they went through, that you understand, and that you are proud of who they have become. Write about the people, places, items, or traits you feel helped your past self to overcome.

4. Next, provide your past self with reassurance and advice. Tell them what they did right in those moments and in moments to come. Tell them how strong they are and the other traits that make them wonderful. Praise them for their ability to move forward in life.

5. After this, provide your past self with some ideas on how to shift their outlook of these experiences into one that allows them to thrive. Some ideas include:

   a. Not getting stuck thinking about the people and actions involved but instead focusing on the actions that can be taken to resolve or to overcome.

   _____
   _____
   _____

   b. Focusing on what can be learned, what can be strengthened, and what can be used as a way to grow.

   _____
   _____
   _____

c. Focusing on forgiveness, either for your own actions or for the actions of others, and how this forgiveness will lift a weight off and allow you to move on.

_____

_____

_____

6. Conclude with more advice and reassurance to your past self.

7. Your second letter will be written/recorded to your future self. Just as in your "Dear Past Self" letter, begin with empathy and care. Explain that you know they may find themselves in moments that are scary or stressful, but you know they can: (a) get through them, and (b) come out stronger for them.

8. Next, provide your future self with advice. Consider using your present insights, as well as the information you shared with your past self about:

   a. Shifting outlooks to see experiences as moments to learn and grow.

   _____

   _____

   _____

   b. How to focus their thoughts in a way that is beneficial and optimistic.

   _____

   _____

   _____

   c. People, places, or items they can turn to for support.

   _____

   _____

   _____

9. Finally, give your future self a pep talk. Let them know what their strengths are, their good qualities, and let them know you believe in them. Think about the person you want to become and use this to build on.

10. Keep these letters close and read/listen to them in those moments when you could use some insider advice or understanding.

Dear Past Self

NOTE Available for download.
See download instructions under the Table of Contents.

Dear Future Self

NOTE Available for download.
See download instructions under the Table of Contents.

SING Like a Rock Star

We all have those moments. Something reminds us of a bad experience from the past, something awful is happening in the present, or we just are having "a moment" and don't even know why. When that happens, we tend to get ourselves stuck on this hamster wheel of bad thoughts. We run and run and run these thoughts in our head, and they just get worse and worse and worse.

What does that lead to?

It leads to us feeling exhausted, worse than before, and it leads to us getting nowhere with no way to move forward.

What can we do about it?

We can SING!

What happens when you hear your favorite song or your favorite artist? It gives you a little jolt of joy, right? Maybe you sing along with the song?

When you're stuck in a moment and can't get off that hamster wheel, think of the jolt of joy your favorite song brings to you and SING! S.I.N.G. SING!

S STOP!

Right there. Stop yourself in the moment. Breathe. Deep, purposeful, slow breaths. Try a grounding technique. Walk away. Get out of the setting you are in, out of your thoughts, and off that hamster wheel.

I Identify the situation.

Sometimes, we get so overwhelmed and flooded with our thoughts that we can't keep track of what's what! Once you've had a moment to stop, to breathe, to ground yourself and gather your thoughts, think. Identify exactly what is going on around you. (Where are you? Who are you with? What is going on?) Use this information to determine what exactly happened to cause your flooded feelings and thoughts.

N Nail down a plan.

Now that you are grounded and have identified what's what, you can figure out a plan of action. What can you do to make yourself feel better in this moment?

If this is something IN your control, you can use your coping strategies to find your calm spot.

If this is something OUT of your control, you can respond in ways that either allow you to accept and move on, or to get out of the situation altogether.

G Go forward, reflect, make changes as needed.

Use those strategies. Change your thinking. Take control, take action, make changes to your action plan as needed, and keep forging ahead until you have reached a place of calm and safety.

Purpose of Exercise:

- Identify situations and events that elevate negative feelings.
- Reflect and determine an action plan to decrease the negative feelings.

What You Will Need:

- *SING Event/Experience Charts*

Directions:

1. Think of a time when you have felt stuck on that hamster wheel.
2. Write the event down.
3. Write how you could have used S.I.N.G. in that moment to help you feel better.
4. Next time you get stuck in the hamster wheel, remember what you wrote down. Remember to S.I.N.G. and use this as a reference to grow from. Add to your notes and strategies for getting off the hamster wheel and for forging ahead like a rockstar.

EVENT/EXPERIENCE

S _____

I _____

N _____

G _____

EVENT/EXPERIENCE

S _____

I _____

N _____

G _____

EVENT/EXPERIENCE

S _____

I _____

N _____

G _____

EVENT/EXPERIENCE

S _____

I _____

N _____

G _____

Choose Your Own Adventure

Have you ever read a "choose your own adventure" book? You know, the ones that allow you to pick from a variety of plots as you watch the story unfold? They have choices like: *"If you want to enter the deep-sea cave, go to page 56. If you want to ride the elephant into the jungle, go to page 45."*

Maybe you have played a video game that allows you to obtain multiple "lives" and to replay "failed" levels/missions?

There is comfort and a little thrill in knowing that, if you didn't like the path you chose, or if you are unsuccessful in defeating a level, you can:

- ☐ ***Replay*** what happened in your mind in order to…

- ☐ ***Reassess*** mistakes/dislikes/alternative actions, etc… so that you can then

- ☐ ***Repair*** with your new understandings, ultimately allowing you to…

- ☐ ***Receive*** the outcome that you desire.

But what if you could do this in real life? What if you could replay an experience in your head in order to better understand what happened from all angles, to look at it from various perspectives, and to figure out what you can reassess in your own reactions and responses to the experience? What if you could reassess how you felt and what you said or did in order to determine what you could have done better, what you could have changed, and what you did right? What if you could use this new information to repair pieces from the experience in order to *receive* the outcome you want?

Of course, we don't have a rewind button that allows us to change our experiences. Still, we can reflect on how we perceive and react to experiences, then we can use this information to modify our thoughts, behaviors, and actions in the future. This helps us to obtain a better outcome in experiences that may arise later.

Purpose of Exercise:

- Reflect on events or experiences, reactions, and perceptions.
- Determine how to shift outcomes by modifying thoughts, behaviors, and actions in the future.

What You Will Need:

- *Choose Your Own Adventure Planning and Alternate Story* page

Choose Your Own Adventure Planning and Alternate Story

DIRECTIONS:

1. Think about an experience you have had that left you feeling unfulfilled, unhappy, or that left you wishing for an alternative conclusion. In your mind, *replay* what happened leading up to, during, and after the experience. Use the prompts in the table below to help:

The Lead Up to the Experience	During the Experience	After the Experience
Where were you?	What happened?	What was the outcome?
Who was with you?	Who was involved?	How did you respond?
What were you doing?	What was the outcome?	What happened as a result of your response?
What were you feeling?	How did you respond?	What were you feeling?

ADDITIONAL NOTES:

2. Now, replay what happened leading up to, during, and after the experience from another person's point of view. Pretend like you were watching it unfold as if you were reading it in a book or watching it in a movie. Try to understand what happened with no emotion, no judgement, and as if it was not going to affect you in any way. Redo the table from the perspective of an onlooker:

The Lead Up to the Experience	**During the Experience**	**After the Experience**
Where was it?	What happened?	What was the outcome?
Who was there?	Who was involved?	How did each player respond?
What was each player doing?	What did they do?	What happened as a result of everyone's response?
What do you think each player was feeling?	What do you think they were feeling?	What do you think each player felt as a result?

ADDITIONAL NOTES:

BUILDING RESILIENCY IN TEENS

3. Next, replay what happened leading to, during, and after the experience from another player's point of view. Perhaps you felt wronged by someone else, or you felt like another person was wronged in the experience. Try to understand what happened from their point of view. Redo the table from the perspective of another key player:

The Lead Up to the Experience	During the Experience	After the Experience
Where were you?	What happened?	What was the outcome?
Who was with you?	Who was involved?	How did you respond?
What were you doing?	What did you do?	What happened as a result of your response?
What were you feeling?	What were you feeling?	What were you feeling?

ADDITIONAL NOTES:

4. Once you feel like you have a solid understanding of the experience from multiple angles, you can reassess your feelings, how they impacted your behaviors and actions, and how this may have impacted the outcome. Consider the following:

How did your feelings during the experience impact your words or actions? Did you say or do anything that you may not have done otherwise? _____

_____

_____

_____

How could you have responded differently? What words, behaviors, or actions do you think may have shifted the story to produce a better conclusion? Try to think of at least 2 alternative ways that you could have responded to produce two different storylines and conclusions.

ALTERNATE STORYLINE #1

ALTERNATE STORYLINE #2

5. Now that you have thought of alternative words and actions, consider what you could do to repair something that may have been broken in the experience. Consider ways to repair pieces from the experience as it relates to…

Another player in the experience	*Some ideas may include:* • Having a conversation with the person and explaining your feelings/why • Writing a letter to the player • Talking to a trusted person about the experience and getting the person's thoughts • Asking for and/or giving an apology
You	*Some ideas may include:* • Positive affirmations • Giving yourself a reward (playing your favorite game, watching your favorite movie, spending a day outside, baking your favorite treat) • Writing yourself a love note, detailing your strengths, what you love about yourself, and why you deserve to feel joyful • Allowing yourself some quiet time alone to relax • Spending time talking and laughing with friends • Self-love activities
Future experiences	*Some ideas may include:* • Thinking about how to better respond to feelings and emotions that arise in you • Thinking about words and actions that you can use in future experiences that would produce a more positive conclusion

6. Finally, use these ideas to create an alternative conclusion. Now that you have a good understanding of the experience and of alternative ways to respond, think about how the use of these alternative thoughts, behaviors, and actions will change the storyline and the ending in experiences that arise in the future.

What will be repaired from this experience? _____

_____

_____

_____

What will be better as a result of your alternative thoughts, actions, and behaviors in future experiences? _____

_____

_____

_____

What will you do to ensure you remember these alternative thoughts, actions, and behaviors for future experiences that arise? _____

_____

_____

_____

Immediate Reflection Notes
Processing Feelings, Emotions, Behaviors, and Actions

You have just completed the section "Processing Feelings, Emotions, Behaviors, and Actions." These activities should have given you a better understanding of your feelings and where they come from, a way to process your emotions in a healthy way, and ideas to regulate in times of stress. Exploring these pieces within yourself is no easy task and you should feel very proud for having done so. While the activities introduced in this section are fresh in your mind, take a minute to reflect on the following:

Interesting discoveries I made about myself are…

_____

_____

_____

Interesting discoveries I made about processing my feelings, emotions, and my subsequent behaviors and actions are…

_____

_____

_____

I am still curious and want to learn more about…

_____

_____

_____

_____

The activities that were most meaningful to me include…

_____

_____

_____

_____

_____

I can extend these ideas into my everyday life by…

_____

_____

_____

_____

Using this new knowledge, my goals for healthy emotional processing include (try to make no more than 3 goals)…

1 _____
_____
_____

2 _____
_____
_____

3 _____
_____
_____

SIGNATURE _____   DATE _____

this will be useful for the check-in reflection intro

Self Check-In Reflection Notes
Processing Feelings, Emotions, Behaviors, and Actions

It has been _____ days since I have completed my reflection on "Processing Feelings, Emotions, Behaviors, and Actions." In that reflection, I set the following emotional processing goals:

1 _____
_____

2 _____
_____

3 _____
_____

If I were to rate myself on how I'm doing when it comes to reaching these goals, I would give myself a (on a scale of 1 to 5: 1=not close at all, 5=super successful)… ☐

A few barriers and snags I've hit along the way are… _____
_____
_____

Some things that have helped me get closer to obtaining my goals are… _____
_____
_____

To keep moving forward, I need… _____
_____

In order to reach my goals, I am committed to… _____
_____

Doodle Page

These pages are for you and you alone. Use them for your own creative self-expression. Write lyrics, make lists, draw, color, whatever your heart desires.

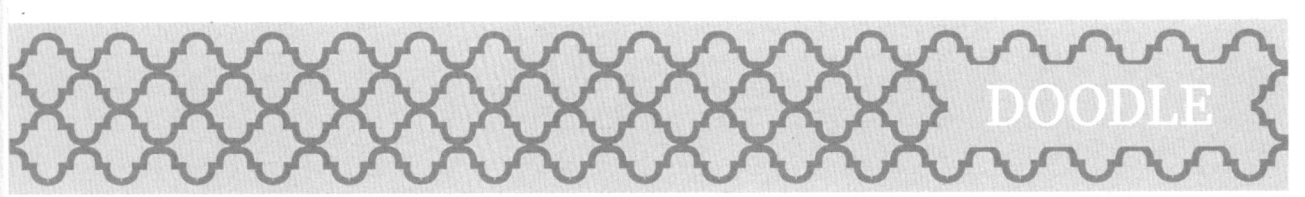

Doodle Page

These pages are for you and you alone. Use them for your own creative self-expression. Write lyrics, make lists, draw, color, whatever your heart desires.

Coping, Grounding, and Calming

Once children and adolescents are empowered with the ability to process emotions in a healthy way, they can then focus on tending to and coping with negative or unpleasant experiences. The application of grounding techniques and healthy coping mechanisms is paramount in overcoming trauma and increasing overall well-being.

The activities in this section are designed to allow for the exploration of various coping tools and techniques. They are vast enough to touch on distinct styles and areas of interest. It is the hope that these activities will illuminate unique strengths and curiosities, which can then be used to create individualized coping plans that suit specific needs.

SPLAT!

Sometimes, we just need a good energy release. Like when you feel super frustrated, invisible, or overwhelmed and just don't know how to verbalize (or may not even want to verbalize) these feelings.

It's important that you don't let these feelings fester. Sometimes we can get them out through reflecting, through talking later, through art, etc. But sometimes, you just need a good "**GRRRRR...** GET IT OUT NOW" moment.

That is where this activity comes in! It provides a quick and fun way to release that pent-up energy, to get the feelings out, and to gain some emotional closure (plus, it's super fun!).

Purpose of Exercise:

- Identify thoughts, experiences, and other pieces that lead to negative feelings.
- Explore a healthy and fun way to release the feelings and energy.

What You Will Need:

- Sharpie markers
- Paper towels
- Water
- An outside wall, tree, or sidewalk

Directions:

1. Take a moment to reflect on what you are feeling. Try to label what you are feeling in the moment. It may be anger, confusion, frustration, sadness, maybe a mixture of many emotions.

2. Think about what is causing these feelings. It may be one major thing, or a ton of small things. But try to recognize what is causing these feelings and match the cause(s) to the feelings you are experiencing.

3. Using your markers, write down exactly what is causing these feelings on a paper towel square. You may write the cause, draw it, and you can even write the feelings attached to this cause if you'd like.

4. If there is more than one cause, write them on separate paper towels. Use as many paper towels as you need to.

5. Once you have each cause written, dunk the paper towel(s) in water. Get them nice and wet.

6. Next, squeeze each towel into a loose ball (do not make it too tight, as it will lose water if you squeeze too hard, and will lose the fun impact in the next step if it is too packed and too dry).

7. Hold the dripping loose towel ball, focus on the designated sidewalk/tree/wall, and throw the towel ball as hard as you can at the wall.

8. You may do this as many times as you'd like.

9. Pay attention to how it makes you feel to rocket that cause far from you, to watch it "SPLAT" onto the wall, to hear the impact of the wet towel crashing into the wall, to have that sense of release and freedom from that cause.

10. Keep this in mind the next time something overwhelms and frustrates you. It is a fun and freeing way to release the energy, release yourself from the cause of negative feelings, and gain emotional closure without having to confront or further experience events or people that may be the cause of these feelings.

Nourishing Nature

When you do something for the greater good that benefits people or things outside of yourself, magic happens. Think about the last time you did something kind. Maybe you held the door for someone or picked up trash off the ground. Maybe you spent a day volunteering or you stuck up for someone being bullied. It can be something big or something small. How did you feel, knowing that your act made the world just a tad bit better? It's amazing, isn't it? The simplest acts of good can produce the best feelings.

Additionally, connecting with nature can create magic! Spending time observing, soaking in, and just being in the moment when you are surrounded by sunshine, trees, wildlife, etc. can evoke warm and positive feelings, a sense of balance, and clarity.

Today's activity involves both of these magical items! You will be making a butterfly feeder in order to provide nourishment for nature, while also allowing nature to nourish you simply by allowing yourself to be present.

ACTIVITY

Purpose of Exercise:

- Explore a calming and confidence-boosting technique.
- Practice the act of doing good/helping.

What You Will Need:

- A kitchen sponge (preferably the kind without the scotch pad side)
- ½ to 1 cup warm water
- ½ to 1 cup sugar
- Scissors
- A shallow dish, bowl, or lid
- Pebbles, sea glass, and other decorative pieces, if desired

Directions:

1. Cut the kitchen sponge into squares and/or other shapes of your choice.
2. Place the pieces (or as many as you can) into the shallow dish, bowl, or lid.
3. Mix the sugar and water together, allowing the sugar to dissolve as much as possible. Do not worry if it does not dissolve completely.
4. Pour the sugar water over the sponges, allowing them to soak in the liquid and allowing some of the liquid to pool inside of the container.

5. If desired, add pebbles, sea glass, or other decorative items.

6. Place the feeder outside during the spring and summer months, preferably near trees, flowers, sunshine, and other attractions for butterflies.

7. Monitor the feeder and add more sugar/water mix as needed. You should see the benefits of your attention and care within a few days, as butterflies pass and recognize this sweet spot for feeding.

8. Continue to watch/replenish throughout the season. As you replenish your feeder or observe from afar while butterflies nourish themselves with the sugar water, be sure to use this time to provide yourself with wellness boosting nourishment, as well. You can do this by:

    a. Taking at least 10-20 minutes outside while replenishing or observing. Focus on your senses in the present moment while doing so. Focus on the sounds, the sights, the feel of sunshine/breezes passing, on the scent of flowers, grass, and trees, etc.

    b. While outside and focusing on your senses and the present moment, also take the time to recognize what you feel as you connect with nature and as you gather sustenance and nourishment from nature.

Swing, Sway, Oscillate, Pendulate

Have you ever seen one of those shows where a magician uses a pendulum (an object attached to a string that slowly sways back and forth) to make someone cluck like a chicken? It's always good for a laugh. The reason why they use a pendulum though, is because the movement, swaying slowly to and fro, can be a peaceful, tranquil, and mesmerizing movement. It can alter one's emotions and thoughts to drift and move from negative to positive and calm.

The calming technique we will explore today involves breathing, timing, and mind swaying back and forth until balance is found. We know that breathing is a powerful tool for calming our minds, bodies, and for preparing our brains to respond to unwelcome situations in a positive way. We are now going to expand on that by adding in the connection of breathing to timing, and by using that connection as we drift back and forth in our minds until we reach a strong mental balance.

ACTIVITY

Purpose of Exercise:

- Practice a simple grounding technique.
- Understand how to pendulate in order to achieve emotional balance.

What You Will Need:

- One piece of string or yarn (about 12-15 inches in length)
- One hardware store nut, heavy bead, or something somewhat weighty that you can easily tie to the string

Directions:

1. To begin, create your pendulum by tying one end of the string to your chosen object. Be sure this object is weighty enough to produce a lasting and smooth swinging motion when you hold the opposite end of the string and gently move your fingers in slight sway motions.
2. Allow the pendulum to move in a gentle swaying motion.
3. As you track the movement of the pendulum, swaying under your control in your fingertips, focus on two things:
   a. The swing and sway of the pendulum
   b. The way your breathing sways with the pendulum
4. Breathe slowly in through your nose for 3 full swings, then out through your mouth for 4 full swings (in 1-2-3… out 1-2-3-4).
5. Allow your mind to drift in this moment. Drift away from any overwhelming or unwelcomed thoughts. Let the sway of the pendulum align with your breathing and move you toward positive thoughts and feelings. Drift toward happiness, positivity, and calm. Welcome and accept these feelings. Stay in this moment.
6. Now, allow your mind to drift in the opposite direction. Let the sway of the pendulum align with your breathing and move you towards the thoughts and feelings that can sometimes make you feel overwhelmed, upset, or uncomfortable. Welcome and accept these feelings. Stay in this moment.
7. Continue to sway back and forth in your mind, between these feelings. Focus on your breathing and how these feelings impact your emotions and your body, and welcome these feelings on both sides of the pendulum swing.
8. Once you are comfortable and accepting of both sides, find your balance, or the center point of your pendulum. Allow your mind to drift to a place where you are comfortable and confident in not feeling 100% well, nor 100% overwhelmed.
9. Reflect on how you feel in this balanced point. Consider the following:
   a. What does your body feel like?
   b. How is your mood?
   c. What emotions are you experiencing?
   d. What emotions did you feel as you swayed back and forth in your mind?
   e. When could this technique be helpful for you?

Strategy Sampling

Purpose of Exercise:

- Explore a variety of grounding, calming, and coping strategies.
- Reflect and create a personal plan for self-soothing and coping.

What You Will Need:

- *Strategy Sampler Card & Reflection* (downloaded, printed double-sided or glued together, and cut out in advance)

Directions:

1. Reflect on how you are feeling at the moment. On a scale from 1-10 (1 being awful, 10 being amazing), where are you? Why do you suppose this is?

2. Cut out the *Strategy Sampler cards*. Explore the various activities written on each card (refer to the "Snap Skills" sampler section of the guidebook for explanation).

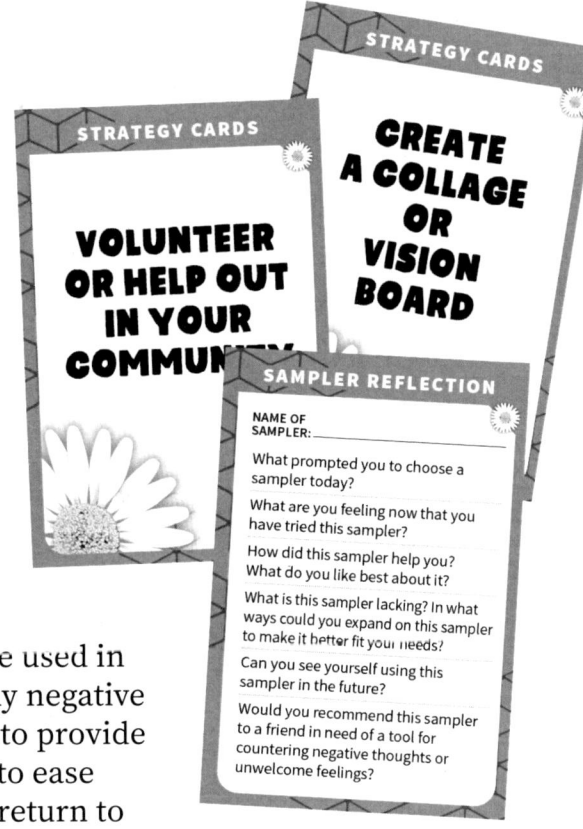

3. These activities are strategies that can be used in moments when you are experiencing any negative or unwelcome feelings. They are meant to provide you with a means to calm, distract, and to ease your body and mind. That way, you can return to "baseline brain." This will allow you to make wise choices about next steps, move forward without allowing these feelings to ruin your day, and just feel better overall.

4. Over the course of the next week or so use this card deck in those moments when you feel you need a means to return to "baseline brain."

5. Make note of the strategies that have the greatest and best impact. If you'd like, you can record the name of those strategies and reflect on the *Strategy Sampler Reflection*, located behind each sampler card.

6. Once you have sampled each of the strategies and determined which work best for you, make note of these. Think about how you will use them in the future. This will allow you to have a concrete master plan of attack when negative and unwelcome feelings or experiences arise.

Strategy Sampler Cards

CARD FRONTS

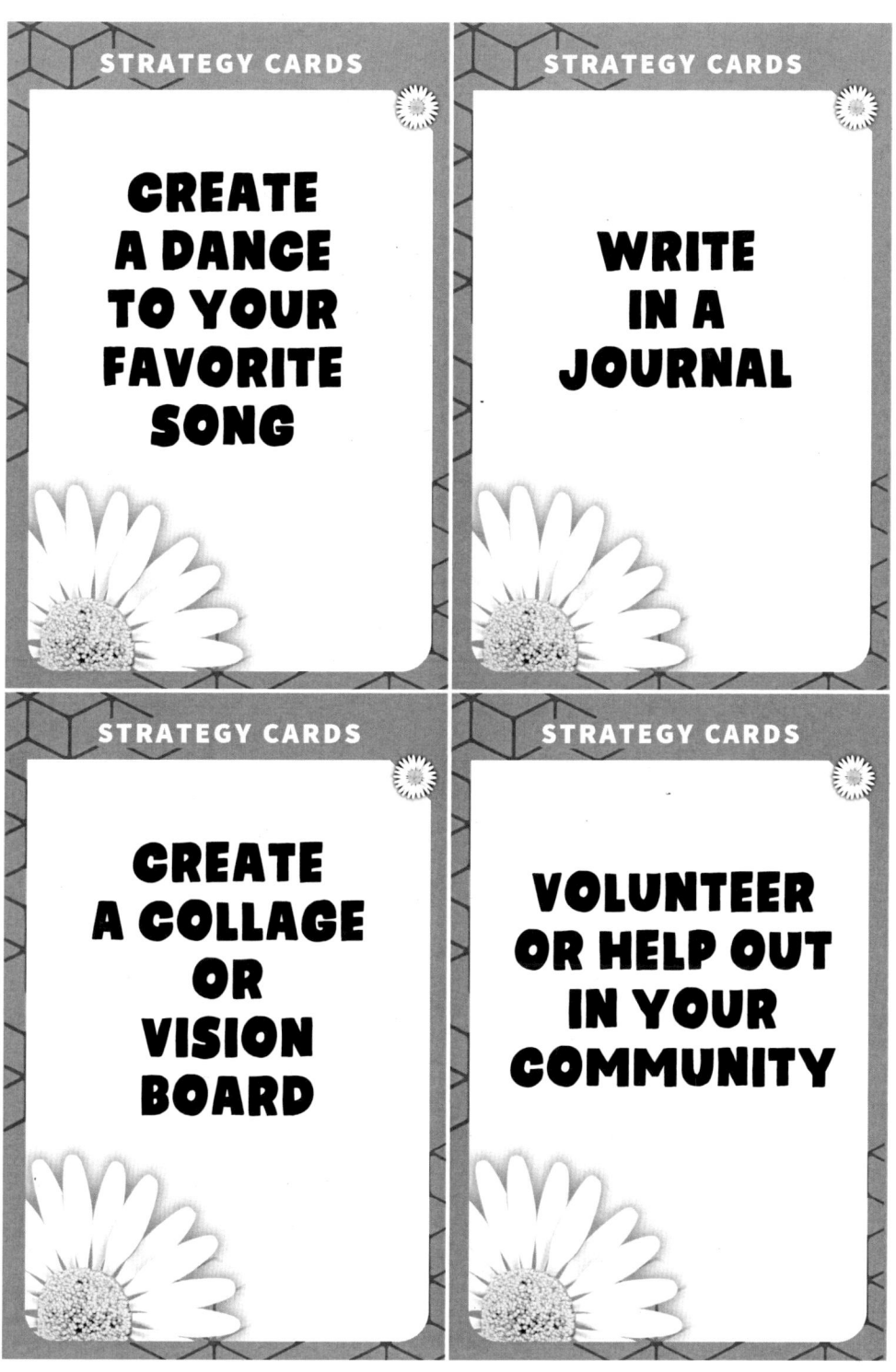

NOTE These are samples. There are 27 *Strategy Sampler Cards* available for download and print. *See download instructions under the Table of Contents.*

Strategy Sampler Cards

CARD BACKS

SAMPLER REFLECTION

NAME OF SAMPLER:_____

What prompted you to choose a sampler today?

What are you feeling now that you have tried this sampler?

How did this sampler help you? What do you like best about it?

What is this sampler lacking? In what ways could you expand on this sampler to make it better fit your needs?

Can you see yourself using this sampler in the future?

Would you recommend this sampler to a friend in need of a tool for countering negative thoughts or unwelcome feelings?

SAMPLER REFLECTION

NAME OF SAMPLER:_____

What prompted you to choose a sampler today?

What are you feeling now that you have tried this sampler?

How did this sampler help you? What do you like best about it?

What is this sampler lacking? In what ways could you expand on this sampler to make it better fit your needs?

Can you see yourself using this sampler in the future?

Would you recommend this sampler to a friend in need of a tool for countering negative thoughts or unwelcome feelings?

SAMPLER REFLECTION

NAME OF SAMPLER:_____

What prompted you to choose a sampler today?

What are you feeling now that you have tried this sampler?

How did this sampler help you? What do you like best about it?

What is this sampler lacking? In what ways could you expand on this sampler to make it better fit your needs?

Can you see yourself using this sampler in the future?

Would you recommend this sampler to a friend in need of a tool for countering negative thoughts or unwelcome feelings?

SAMPLER REFLECTION

NAME OF SAMPLER:_____

What prompted you to choose a sampler today?

What are you feeling now that you have tried this sampler?

How did this sampler help you? What do you like best about it?

What is this sampler lacking? In what ways could you expand on this sampler to make it better fit your needs?

Can you see yourself using this sampler in the future?

Would you recommend this sampler to a friend in need of a tool for countering negative thoughts or unwelcome feelings?

NOTE These are samples. There are 27 *Strategy Sampler Cards* available for download and print. *See download instructions under the Table of Contents.*

Serenity Strings

Purpose of Exercise:

- Explore calming the mind with abstract art.

What You Will Need:

- Various colors of thread
- Glue
- Brush (for evenly spreading the glue)
- Paper, inflated balloon, or a plastic bottle/bowl (paper if you would like to create a picture and balloon, bottle or bowl if you would like to create a sculpture)

Directions:

1. Cut a good amount of thread in your chosen colors. You may choose colors that symbolize your emotions, or colors that are simply appealing to you.
2. Using a brush, evenly coat the platform on which you will be creating your serenity strings art. This may be paper, an inflated balloon, or a plastic bottle or bowl. Try to ensure the entire platform is covered with a good and even amount of glue.
3. One at a time, place the thread onto the glued area. Allow the thread to swivel, swirl and loop, and overlap, creating a maze of abstract, multi-colored beauty.
4. If needed, carefully brush more glue onto the thread as you continue to add to your work of art.
5. Breathe, focus on your art, and observe as the threads layer and loop to create something of beauty.
6. When you feel you are done, allow the threads to dry.
7. If using a balloon, pop and deflate once dried.
8. Reflect on how this project made you feel during and after creation. Consider how this project could be useful when you are feeling negative thoughts.

Secret Silent Whisper Shout

Have you ever had one of those moments? A moment where you want to shout something from the rooftops, but at the same time, keep it under wraps? It may be expressing your feelings about a situation or event. It may be words you want to share with someone but can't. It may be secret affirming words you want to keep to yourself but want to be reminded of when needed.

This activity will allow you to do just that: express something that you'd like to get out either in a whisper, a shout, or in a way that is entirely hidden to the rest of the world, with only you knowing that it is there in plain sight. Also, you will be doing so by creating art in a tranquil and soothing manner.

Purpose of Exercise:

- Express emotions in an emotionally safe and artistic way.
- Explore a calming and soothing strategy.

What You Will Need:

- 1 white crayon
- Paper
- Paintbrushes (various sizes, if possible)
- Watercolor paints

Directions:

1. Reflect on something you would like to make your focal point in this activity. It could be an experience, a feeling, a person, words that resonate with you, whatever you would like to share without sharing.

2. Using words, pictures, symbols, lines, or any form that you would like, use the white crayon to express this focal point on paper. Try to press firmly. Focus on your breathing and on the energy flowing from you onto the paper. (Keep in mind that your work will not be visible on the white paper.)

3. Continue to focus on freely and nonjudgmentally allowing your feelings about this focal point to flow out of you and quietly onto the paper.

4. When finished, you may choose to either:
   a. Allow your artwork to shout loudly at the world
   b. Allow your artwork to whisper to the world
   c. Allow your artwork to remain secret and silent with only you knowing it is out there in plain sight

5. Once you have chosen how you would like to express this artwork to the world, gather the watercolors and begin to brush strokes in a manner that matches your choice (see steps 6-8 to learn more). Focus on your breaths and on the calming feeling that comes from allowing your energy to flow onto the paper with each brushstroke.

6. In order to shout loudly, you may use the watercolors in a vibrant and loud way. This involves using bold colors, less water, and more color.

7. In order to whisper, you may choose to use more muted colors, or by using more water and less paint.

8. In order to keep this secret in the open but only obvious to you, do not use watercolor or simply use very pale colors and plenty of water.

9. When finished, reflect on how this activity impacted your feelings. What does your body feel like after completing this? How did it impact your thinking and your emotions? Do you feel more relaxed? Do you feel accomplished? Do you feel empowered or like you have a weight lifted off your shoulders?

10. Consider how this activity could be used in future moments when you need to get something out.

We've Got the Beat

Have you ever seen a military movie? Perhaps you've noticed that soldiers often have a beat or a chant they march or run to in these movies. It helps to keep them pushing, puts them into a rhythmic trance, and allows them to push through the pain in order to achieve their goal.

Maybe you have experienced something similar. If not, you can test this idea out with a few simple actions! Try dancing without music, then again with music that carries a good beat. Or, try working out or going for a run without music, then again with music that carries a fast paced and uplifting beat. If you'd rather do something less physically active and more mentally activating, try playing something with a noticeable and entrancing beat as you study. Some people find that studying to a slow and calming beat allows them to find their own rhythm or beat and to focus more!

Purpose of Exercise:

- Use music and beats to express emotions.
- Use music and beats to find balance and calm when needed.

These next two activities spotlight beats. They entail creating your own rhythm or beat and finding your own flow in order to:

1. Express yourself through music
2. Place yourself into a calming trance and to achieve balance

What You Will Need:

- An "instrument" as defined in step 1

Directions:

1. Choose an instrument at hand. This could be:
    a. A pencil that you drum on your leg or a desk
    b. Tapping your fingers
    c. Clicking your tongue
    d. Tapping your toes on the ground
    e. Any other creative means you can find to create a rhythm

2. This first activity involves using a beat to express yourself. Try one or more of the suggestions that follow:
    a. Reflect on what you are feeling right now. What emotions or feelings best describe where you are in the moment?
    b. Use your instrument to create a beat that represents what you are feeling. Continue to play this beat as long as you would like.
    c. Experiment with other beats in order to express other emotions that you have felt. You may want to create a beat for feelings and emotions such as:
        i. Happy
        ii. Sad
        iii. Afraid
        iv. Confused
        v. Angry
        vi. Excited
        vii. Victorious
    d. Consider creating a beat to express yourself and focus on calm whenever you are experiencing unwelcome thoughts.

3. The next activity involves using a beat to find calm and balance. In a sense, you will create a beat to put yourself into a trance, allow your mind to drift from the present, and focus on the rhythm in order to step away from an unwelcome feeling or experience in order to soothe and calm yourself.

Bon Voyage!

Purpose of Exercise:

- Strengthen the ability to take a mini-mind vacation when you need a break.
- Use imagery to find calm.

They say a picture is worth a thousand words. Pictures capture the beauty, emotion, memories, and magic of any given focal point at any given moment. In this activity, you will use a picture to take a mini-mind vacation and transport yourself to a place that you desire to be.

What You Will Need:

- *Bon Voyage* short answers
- A picture as defined in step 1

Directions:

Search online, in books, on your phone, or other photo-bearing platform. Scan until you find a photo that both (a) captures your attention, and (b) is a source of pleasure. Take a moment to consider the following questions:

1. What is this photo of?
   _____

2. What is it about this photo that captures your attention?
   _____
   _____

3. What do you think the photographer was trying to capture with this image?
   _____
   _____

4. If the photo has people in it, what do you think they are feeling? Why?
   _____
   _____

5. If you were in this photo, what would you be feeling? Why?

   _____
   _____
   _____

6. Close your eyes and put yourself in this photo. One at a time, focus on your senses. What would you hear? Feel (temperature, when touching an object in the photo, etc.)? Taste? See? Smell?

   _____
   _____
   _____

MY PHOTO TITLE

7. A picture may be worth a thousand words but what 5 words would you use to describe this picture?

   _____
   _____
   _____
   _____

8. How does escaping into the world of this photo make you feel emotionally? What positive feelings and emotions come from doing this?

   _____
   _____
   _____
   _____

9. Keep this photograph in the back of your mind. Come to this place whenever you need a mini-mind vacation.

Lighthouse Beacon Flexes and Senses

Imagine your thoughts and feelings as a lighthouse. Further, picture your behaviors and actions as a boat, and picture outside occurrences and events as the ocean.

During calm waters, a boat can easily spot the lighthouse and coast to safety. However, during rough waters, waves create great difficulty for a boat to find safety.

If you are experiencing calm, positive, and neutral experiences, then your behaviors and actions will follow suit. Your thoughts and feelings are bright and can easily provide you with a sense of safety and positivity. On the other hand, if you are getting flooded with rough experiences or having a ton of heavy-hitting events thrown your way, it can impact your ability to: (a) maintain a clear vision of your thoughts, (b) figure out how to correctly maneuver your behaviors and actions, and (c) arrive at feelings of safety.

When this happens, it is important to keep our sights on that guiding beacon of light and allow that light to focus on us.

This next activity is split into two sections.

The first involves placing a spotlight on various parts of your body so you may (a) recognize what you are feeling physically, and (b) release tension in order to anchor and refocus.

The second involves placing a spotlight on individual pieces of the present in order to anchor and refocus.

These activities can be done anytime, anywhere.

THOUGHTS AND FEELINGS

THINGS WE CANNOT CONTROL

BEHAVIORS AND ACTIONS

ACTIVITY

Purpose of Exercise:

- Explore two simple grounding techniques.
- Focus on parts instead of the whole to gain clarity and calm.

What You Will Need:

No materials truly necessary for this but if you would like, you may use:

- scents such as lotions, essential oils, baking extracts
- "feeler" items such as Velcro, cotton, fidgets, soft stone, shaving cream
- tastes such as mints, cinnamon, fruits, sweet/sour/salty/spicy varieties
- music or calming sounds apps

Directions:

Lighthouse Beacon Flexes

1. Imagine a lighthouse beacon is slowly pivoting its beam on various parts of your body. For each body part identified/in the spotlight below, take a slow 10 seconds to flex and squeeze it as hard as you can. Be sure to slowly breathe in through your nose and out through your mouth as you flex.

2. After 10 seconds, slowly release and breathe out, paying particular attention to how this release feels.

LIGHTHOUSE BEACON SPOTLIGHT ON...

Arms	Stomach/Core	Upper legs	Shoulders
Hands	Wrists	Toes	Calves

Lighthouse Beacon Senses

1. Shift the beacon of light from your body to your five senses. Remind yourself to be in the present moment and only focus on one sense at a time. If any other thoughts enter, allow them to drift away and wait until you are ready for them.

2. For each sense identified/in the spotlight below, take a slow 10 seconds to focus on that sense. It helps to close your eyes during the senses not involving sight, as that act can enhance your other senses.

3. Remember to breathe slowly in through your nose and out through your mouth as you focus on your senses in the present moment.

LIGHTHOUSE BEACON SPOTLIGHT ON...

Sight	Sounds	Taste	Smell	Touch
EXAMPLES...				
Color Shape Movement Contrast	Loud Soft Human/Nature Machine	Salty Spicy Sweet Sour	Natural Manmade Calming Energizing	Cold Hot Smooth Hard

Immediate Reflection Notes
Coping, Grounding, and Calming

You have just completed the section "Coping, Grounding, and Calming." The activities in this section were meant to provide you with exploratory tools and techniques that will help you cope with stressful situations, ground yourself, and reach a state of calm. While the activities demonstrated are just a few stars in an entire galaxy of tools and techniques, they should give you a good sense of what works best for you as a uniquely wonderful person with uniquely wonderful skills and preferences. While these tools and techniques are fresh in your mind, take a moment to reflect on the following:

Interesting discoveries I made about myself are…

_____

_____

_____

Some tools and techniques that best match who I am include….

_____

_____

_____

I am still curious and want to learn more about tools and techniques that incorporate… (i.e., art, music, movement, the 5 senses, nature, etc.)

_____

_____

_____

_____

I can incorporate these tools and techniques into my everyday life by…

_____

_____

_____

_____

Some tools and techniques that I can create on my own include…

_____

_____

_____

_____

Using this new knowledge, my goals for using coping, grounding, and calming techniques include (try to make no more than 3 goals)…

1 _____

_____

_____

2 _____

_____

_____

3 _____

_____

_____

SIGNATURE _____   DATE _____

* this will be useful for the check-in reflection intro

Self Check-In Reflection Notes
Coping, Grounding, and Calming

It has been _____ days since I have completed my reflection on "Coping, Grounding, and Calming." In that reflection, I set the following goals for using tools and techniques:

1 _____
_____

2 _____
_____

3 _____
_____

If I were to rate myself on how I'm doing when it comes to reaching these goals, I would give myself a (on a scale of 1 to 5: 1=not close at all, 5=super successful)… ☐

A few barriers and snags I've hit along the way are… _____
_____
_____

Some things that have helped me get closer to obtaining my goals are… _____
_____
_____

To keep moving forward, I need… _____
_____

In order to reach my goals, I am committed to… _____
_____
_____

Doodle Page

These pages are for you and you alone. Use them for your own creative self-expression. Write lyrics, make lists, draw, color, whatever your heart desires.

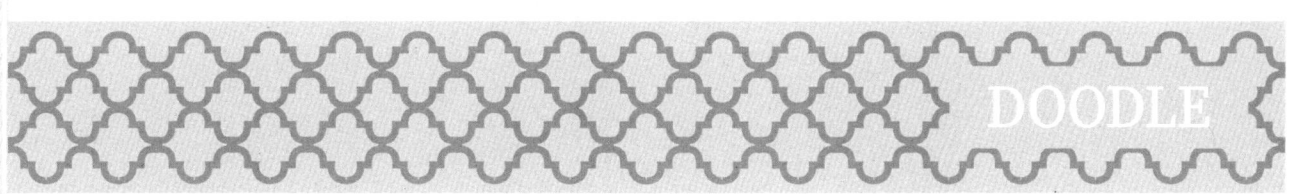

Doodle Page

These pages are for you and you alone. Use them for your own creative self-expression. Write lyrics, make lists, draw, color, whatever your heart desires.

Doodle Page

These pages are for you and you alone. Use them for your own creative self-expression. Write lyrics, make lists, draw, color, whatever your heart desires.

Confidence-Boosting, Strength, and Resilience

—

This final section serves to strengthen resiliency and boost sense of self. Adapting and rebounding from adversity, treating challenges and disappointments as opportunities, and developing an unwavering belief in oneself, are some of the main attributes in overcoming trauma and living prosperously.

These activities focus on challenging negative self-talk, developing productive and affirming perceptions of self and of experiences, and practicing gratitude and positive thinking.

Included in this section are reflective exercises that focus on both internal and external sources of strength and encouragement. These activities are meant to serve as a catalyst for developing a positive mindset, grit, and a lifelong ability to bounce back from adversity.

Playlist Twist

Purpose of Exercise:

- Explore feelings and thoughts through creative mediums.

What You Will Need:

- A quiet place to think about the prompts below

Directions:

1. Reflect on the previous activities.
2. Think of your current top 5 favorite songs. Try to find songs that run the gamut of tone, speed, rhythm, mood, etc.
3. Play those songs in your head.
4. Instead of paying attention to the lyrics, think about the rhythm and beat of these songs.
5. Choose one with a beat and rhythm that best matches your mood, feelings, thoughts, and emotions in the present moment.
6. Replay this song, without lyrics, in your head. As you do so, try to come up with lyrics to describe your current mood, feelings, thoughts, and/or emotions to match the song's rhythm and beat.
7. These lyrics do not need to rhyme or perfectly match the song; in fact, they do not even really need to make sense! Use this time to have fun, be creative, and express yourself without worry.
8. If you want to take this hit song from gold to platinum status, you could even come up with dance moves to your musical remake!
9. Once you have completed this, take a moment to reflect. Ask yourself questions like:
    a. How did channeling my mood, feelings, thoughts and/or emotions for something creative change my outlook?
    b. How did channeling my innermost elements for making this song help me to better understand myself?
    c. If you chose to create dance moves to match your new song, ask yourself: How did creativity and movement effect my mood, feelings, thoughts, and/or emotions?

Personal Bill of Rights

The United States Bill of Rights contains the first ten amendments to our Constitution. It guarantees certain rights and liberties to every person who lives in the nation.

While these rights are specific to those who live in the United States, there are certain other rights that we as humans are deserving of. Let's explore some of these rights.

Purpose of Exercise:

- Identify and reflect on personal rights and liberties.

What You Will Need:

- *Personal Bill of Rights*

Directions:

1. Read the rights that you are deserving of in the *Personal Bill of Rights* on the next page.
2. Write in 3 other rights you feel you are deserving of in the space provided.
3. When needed, reread these rights to yourself. If possible, look in a mirror as you recite these rights of which you are deserving.
4. If you, at any moment, feel as if these rights are being violated, speak with a trusted adult. Create a plan together to ensure these rights are once again provided to you.

Personal Bill of Rights

I have the right to surround myself with supportive and kind people who see my strengths and who encourage me.

I have the right to ignore and steer clear of anyone who makes me feel like I am "less than" or undeserving, or who makes me feel like I cannot accomplish my goals.

I have the right to do things I enjoy. I have the right to have fun, explore positive and healthy things, and spend time doing what makes me happy.

I have the right to be kind to myself, ensure I have everything I need to be healthy and happy, and be happy with the person that I am.

I have the right to feel respected by others. If someone disrespects me, I have the right to tell them I deserve better, will not tolerate disrespect, and to walk away.

I have the right to _____
_____

I have the right to _____
_____

I have the right to _____
_____

I have the right to love, to be loved, and to be proud of the person I am.

Kintsugi Bowl

Kintsugi bowls are artistic representations of the imperfections, broken pieces, and bad experiences that can be turned around to become things of beauty instead of things of shame or anger. Originating in Japan, these bowls are literally broken shards of a bowl, glued together with beautiful gold repairing glue, and transformed into a stunning work of art.

Purpose of Exercise:

- Reflect on experiences and the positivity derived from them.
- Strengthen self-esteem and ability to recognize strengths.

What You Will Need:

- One clay, ceramic, or paper bowl
- If using clay or ceramic bowl:
    - One plastic baggie big enough to hold the bowl
    - Hammer
    - Strong glue (preferably gold in color)
- Paint, glitter, and decorative materials
- If using paper bowl:
    - Scissors
    - Strong glue (preferably gold in color)
    - Paint, glitter, and decorative materials

Directions for Clay or Ceramic Bowl:

1. Place the bowl inside of the plastic baggie and zip shut.
2. Carefully tap the bowl with the hammer, making large breaks in the bowl. Try not to create too many breaks or too small of breaks as this will make putting the bowl back together very difficult.

3. Using the paint, glitter, and decorative materials, decorate each piece of the bowl. You can decorate them to be similar, different, representative or symbolic, whatever you would like.

4. Carefully glue the pieces back together, creating the bowl again. This may take some time, patience, and re-gluing.

5. If you cannot find gold glue, you may choose to sprinkle glitter onto the glue before it dries.

Directions for Paper Bowl:

1. Cut the bowl into pieces with your scissors. They can be various shapes, sizes, swirly, straight, or jagged cuts, anything you'd like. Make the pieces almost like puzzle pieces.

2. Using the paint, glitter, and decorative materials, decorate each piece of the bowl. You can decorate them to be similar, different, representative or symbolic, whatever you would like.

3. Carefully glue the pieces back together, creating the bowl again. This may take some time, patience, and re-gluing.

4. If you cannot find gold glue, you may choose to sprinkle glitter onto the glue before it dries.

Keep your finished work of art as a reminder. The flaws, bad experiences, or imperfections you may see within yourself only serve to make you a more unique and stunning person. Someone to be admired, respected, and looked at with awe and inspiration.

My Personal Slogan

Finish the slogan:

"America runs on _____."™

"Snap, Crackle, _____!"™

"Melts in your mouth, not in your _____."™

Pretty fun, right? Did you know the answers immediately?

A slogan is sort of like a brand's mantra. It is a short and memorable phrase that captures the attention of consumers and makes them more likely to choose that product. A good slogan can be very powerful. Even if you don't know much about a specific brand, you are more likely to reach for it if you are familiar with the slogan as it tends to pop into your mind when you are shopping for a particular item.

Just as you may unwittingly hear a product's slogan in the back of your mind when considering which brand to choose, a mantra or a personal slogan has the power to impact your emotions and your confidence without you realizing it!

Purpose of Exercise:

- Create mood/confidence/strength-boosting mantras.

What You Will Need:

- *My Personal Slogans* activity page

Directions:

1. Reflect on the previous activities.
2. Consider the provided scenarios.
3. Using lyrics, words you've heard in movies or books, or something you have thought of yourself, come up with one strong, short phrase for each. Be sure that these phrases are personally moving to you and are powerful for you. (See provided examples.)
4. In moments where you are feeling as the scenarios describe, remind yourself of these personal slogans. Keep them in the back of your mind and allow them to change your thinking into something more powerful, boosting, and helpful.
5. Repeat these personal slogans to yourself over and over. Eventually, they will become just as powerful as a strong business slogan.

Mantra Examples

"I choose Happiness."

"I choose to be GRATEFUL."

"I am loved."

"I will SUCCEED."

"I am worthy."

"This too, shall pass."

"I am strong, fearless, and brave."

"I let go of NEGATIVES and CHOOSE POSITIVITY."

"I am capable of great things."

"I am awesome."

My Personal Slogans

When I'm feeling nervous, anxious, or worried, I will remind myself...

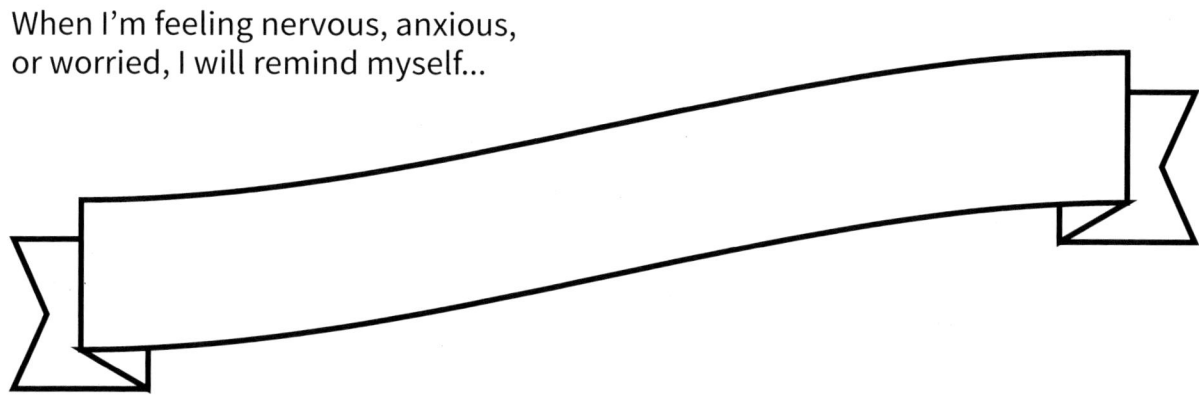

When I'm feeling unsure, unconfident, or undeserving, I will remind myself...

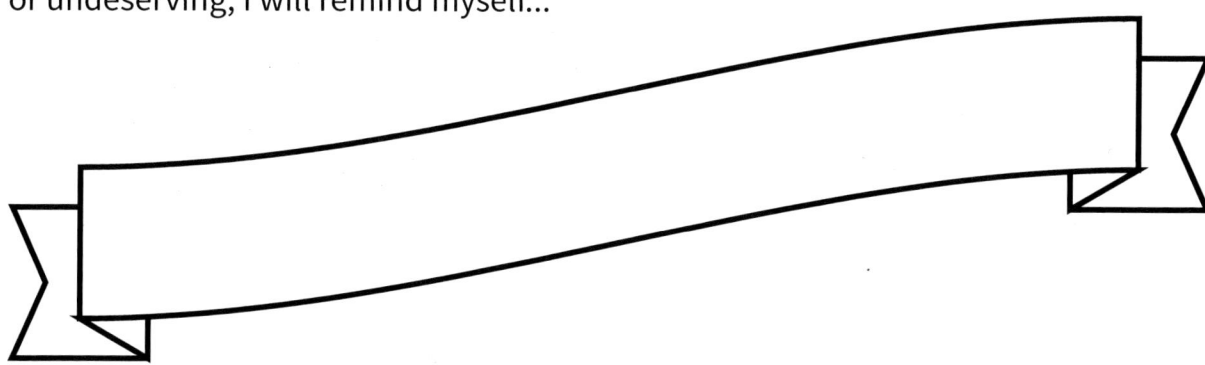

When I'm feeling generally icky and don't know why, I will remind myself...

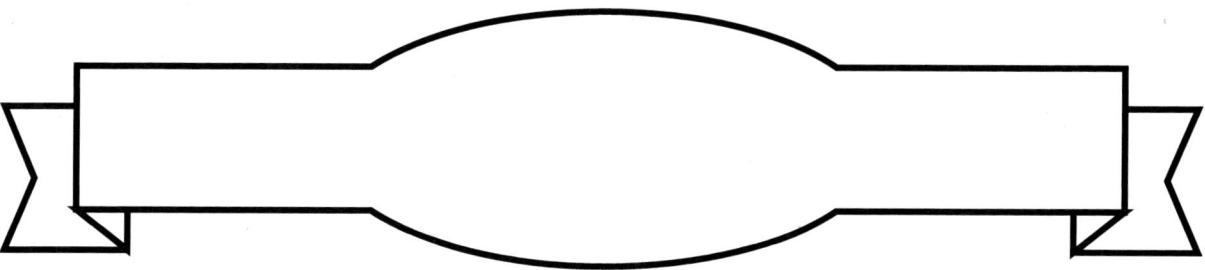

Catch of the Day

Everyone needs someone sometimes. In fact, there have been countless songs written about that! We all need a strong support net of people who we trust, care about us, and give us the strength to get through the tough times. It's human nature. We need to know we have people who will catch us should we fall, and vice versa.

In addition to the knowledge that we have a support net, we all need to hone in on the little daily blips of positivity, big and small, in order to maintain optimal wellness. In fact, focusing on the small moments of gratitude increases our mental, physical, and emotional wellness in both the short- and long-term.

In this activity, you will explore your support net. You will reflect and consider everyone who you can count on when times get tough. You will also focus on daily moments of positivity that you can capture and hold onto.

Purpose of Exercise:

- Identify the trusted people and places that I can turn to when in need.
- Reflect on small moments of gratitude.

What You Will Need:

- Decorative fish netting (found at craft stores or online)
- Wooden or plastic clothes hangers (about 15, to start)
- Hot glue (optional)
- Seashells or sea glass (optional)
- Cut out sea shapes (fish, sea shells)

Directions:

1. Hang the fish netting on a wall (or on a poster board, then taped to a wall) that you frequently pass by. Make sure this is a space where you can keep this netting up for a long period of time.

2. If desired, glue pieces of seashells and/or sea glass to the netting and to the ends of your clothes hangers for added coastal color and tranquility.

3. Clip the clothes hangers on the net. You do not need to be strategic, just anywhere you feel you'd like to clip them.

4. Take a moment to reflect on your support net. Who are those people who you trust, who have your best interests at heart, and who you know you can rely on either for an ear to bend, to keep you healthy and safe, for good advice, for a good laugh, or for any other need you would want to have fulfilled?

5. Write the names of each support net catch on one of the fish sea shapes and clip to one of the clothes hangers.

6. Next, consider one thing you are grateful for today. This could be a person, an experience, an item, a sense, something big or small, but one thing that you are grateful for today and in this moment.

7. Write this thing on a shell sea shape and clip onto your net.

8. Each day, add to this net. Think of one person who is in your support net and add to your "fish catches," or think of one thing you are grateful for and add to your "shell collection."

9. Keep this net up and revisit it daily as a reminder.

BUILDING RESILIENCY IN TEENS

Fish Sea Shapes

DIRECTIONS: Write the names of people within your support net inside of these fish shapes. Cut and hang as appropriate.

Sea Shell Shapes

DIRECTIONS: Write one thing that you are grateful for each day inside of these sea shells. Cut and hang as appropriate.

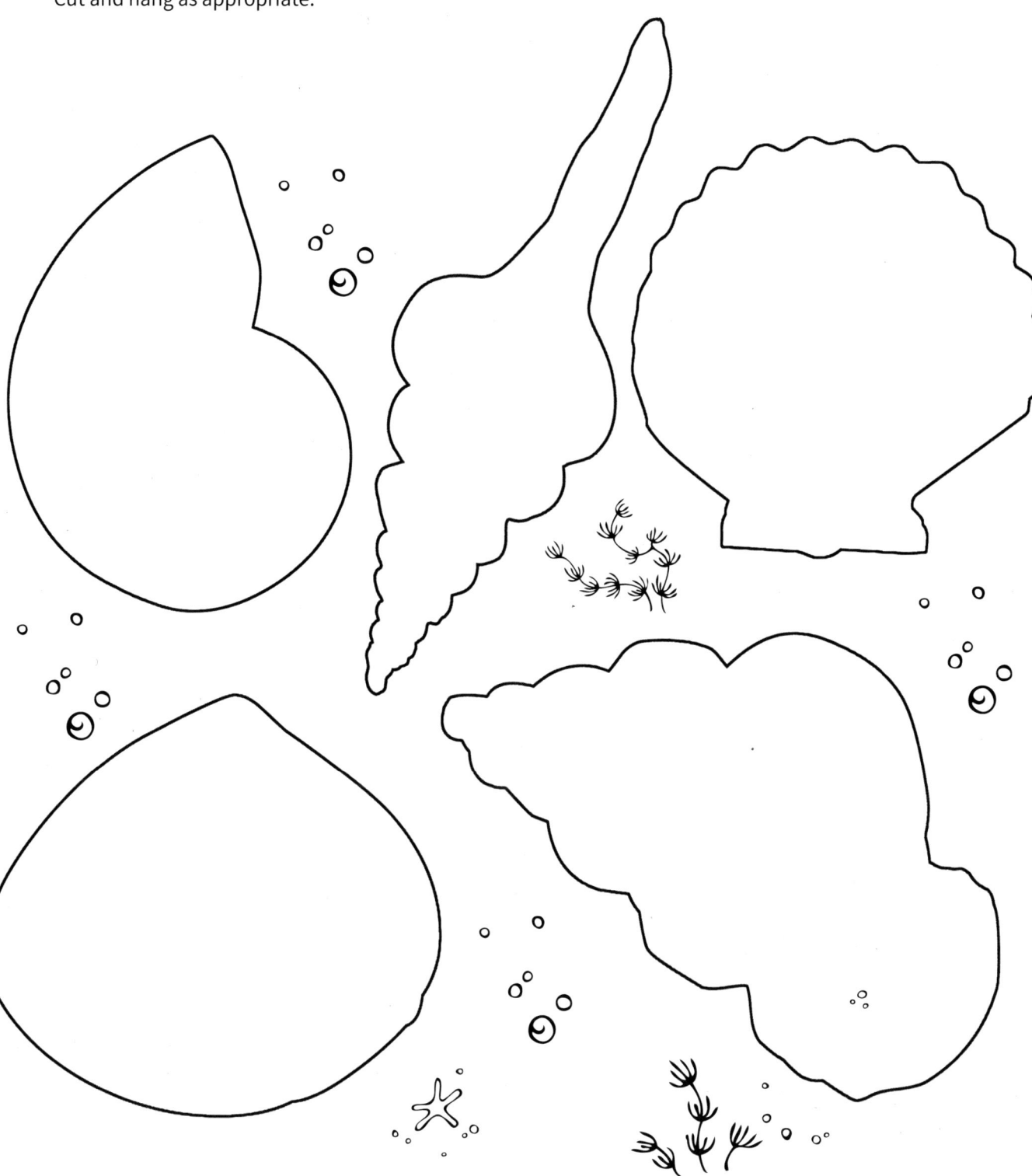

Back to the Future

Our past does not necessarily dictate our future, however, our experiences and how we choose to respond to them certainly play a role in the person we become.

We can choose to see our experiences, good and bad, as opportunities to learn, grow, and make changes to reach our goals. The people we encounter, the moments we remember, the failures that become successes with hard work, and every building block we keep in our memories help to shape us. The way in which we are shaped, though, is based on how we choose to view and use these blocks.

For this activity, you will be looking at your past, reflecting on your present, and looking ahead to your future. You will consider all of the building blocks (significant people and events in your life) that led you to the person you are now, as well as how you can use these blocks, and those to come, to create the future you desire.

Purpose of Exercise:

- Determine how to channel what we have learned and experienced to create the future that we want.
- Gain confidence in self and in your ability to reach future hopes and goals.

What You Will Need:

- Pictures and/or drawings of childhood, past experiences, family members, friends, and other memories that shaped you
- Pictures and/or drawings that reflect you in the present
- Magazines that you do not mind cutting up
- Poster board or cardboard box (shoe, cereal, etc.)
- Scissors
- Glue

Directions:

1. Take a look at the pictures and drawings both past and the present. Reflect on them, conjure up the memories, and retell your story as you look through them.

2. Choose the pictures you feel are most representative of you, of the people and experiences that have shaped you, and that just make you feel good.

3. If you would like, cut the pictures to hone in on the focal points within them.

4. Next, browse through the magazines at hand. Look for words, pictures, colors, and symbols that you feel represent the person you want to be or the life you want to lead. Maybe they are words like "strong," "funny," or "fearless." Maybe they are photos of the beach or of a football. Whatever they may be, cut the pictures out that you feel resonate with your future goals and aspirations.

5. As you browse the magazines, if you find any words, pictures, or symbols that represent either your past or present self, you may cut them out as well and add them to your collection.

6. Using either the poster board or cardboard box, glue the photos onto specific sides.
    a. For the past, glue your photos onto the left side of the poster board (if using poster board), or glue them to one side of the box (if using a box).
    b. For the present, glue your photos onto the middle of the poster board (if using poster board), or glue them to another side of the box (if using a box).
    c. For the future, glue your photos onto the right side of the poster board (if using poster board), or glue them to another side of the box (if using a box).

7. Take a minute to look at your work of art. Reflect on the photos and the various elements that have created you. Think about the following:
    a. How did these past experiences and people help lead you to who you are now?
    b. What past experiences and people (both positive and not so positive) led to your strengths and traits?
    c. What does the "future side" of your artwork say about the person you want to become?
    d. Think of 3 concrete things you can start doing now to reach your future goals. For example, if you want to become a nurse, what should you focus on the most in your schoolwork? If you want to become a faster runner, what ways could you train your legs to move quicker? What kinds of people should you surround yourself with? What should you do if you experience any setbacks or unsupportive people?

My Refreshing Cycle Plans

Do you remember learning about the 4 stages of the water cycle in class? Here's a quick refresher:

☐ **Condensation** – water droplets gather together to form clouds

☐ **Precipitation** – clouds get too heavy and need to release some water in the form of rain or snow

☐ **Collection** – rain and melted snow collects in streams, rivers, oceans, lakes, and land

☐ **Evaporation** – the sun heats water, turning it into a vapor, which can then be lifted back into the sky to form clouds

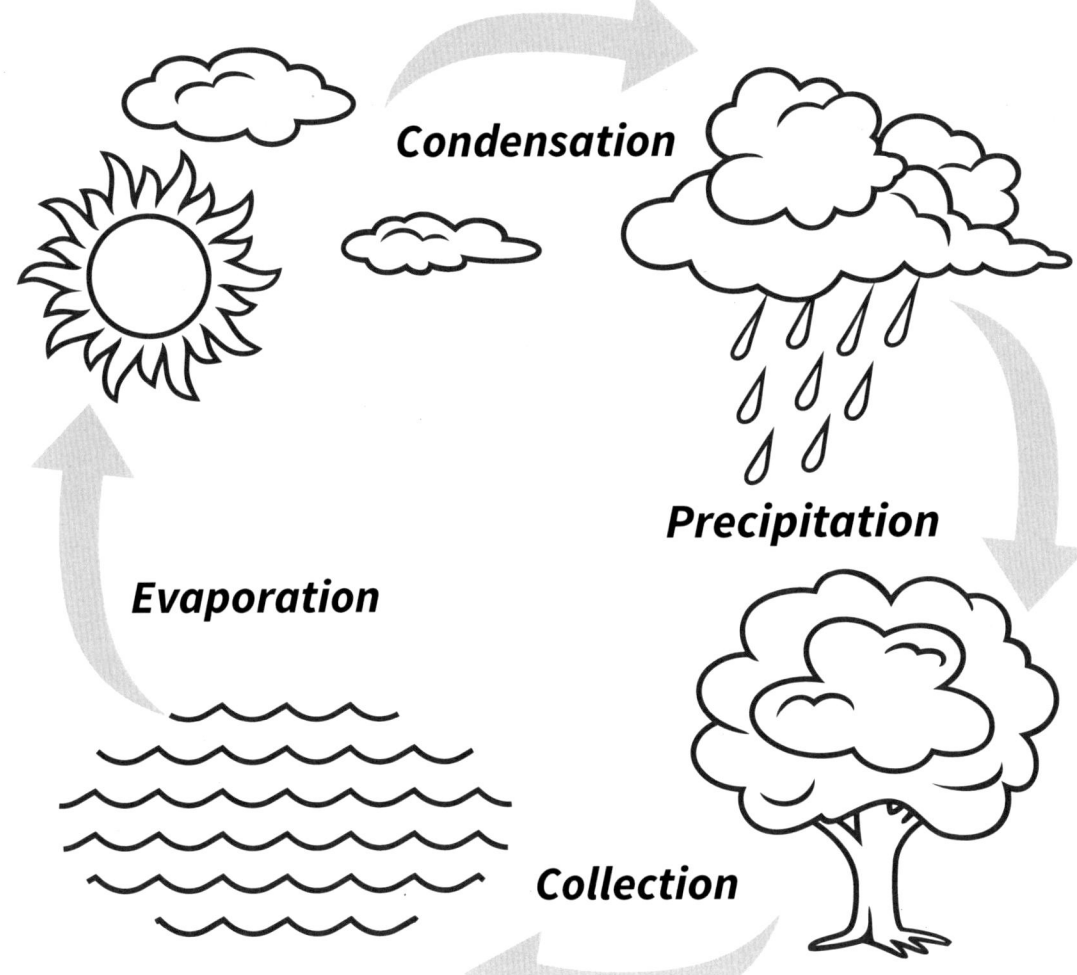

This next activity is sort of like the water cycle. Instead of refreshing water, though, we will be thinking about our thoughts and emotions, how they impact our behaviors and actions, and how we can use this to create a refreshing, healthy, and helpful cycle that can be used again and again.

The four cycles of this activity align with the water cycle in this way:

☐ *Release*

☐ *Relax*

☐ *Realign*

☐ *Ready*

Release

Let's start by thinking about the stage of **precipitation.** Have you ever been caught in a rain or snowstorm? Well, your mind and body kind of do the same thing when you are flooded with negative or unwanted feelings and emotions! It takes over and you just don't know what to do with all that energy! You might want to cry, scream, hit, or get away from everyone. You need a ***release.***

Just as clouds release the heavy water when it's filled to the max, you need to release that energy that is building up inside.

You can do this in a variety of ways, including:

- Write down what is flooding you, then rip the paper up.
- Punch or scream into a pillow.
- Exercise.
- Dance to fast and loud music.
- Do jumping jacks, run in place, or do air karate moves.

Relax

The next stage of the water cycle is **collection.** This is where water collects in land and water. Like water collects itself, the ***relax*** stage entails you collecting yourself. This is where you really pay attention to your breathing. You want your breaths to be calming and soothing. That way, your body can slow down. This allows your brain to start taking charge over the feelings and emotions that were flooding you.

You can do this in a variety of ways, including:

- Take deep and purposeful breaths.
- Meditate.
- Practice yoga or mindfulness.
- Do guided visualization.
- Use imagery/going to a safe and comfortable place in your mind.

Realign

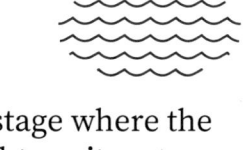

The next stage in the water cycle is **evaporation.** Just as this is the stage where the sun heats water and lightens it up to become a gas, the ***realign*** stage is where you allow your negative feelings and emotions to vaporize into something else. It is where you calm down enough to allow your brain to take control back from the flooding. You should feel super calm and lighter after realigning. Your brain should feel focused and ready to move forward in a healthy way.

You can do this in a variety of ways, including:

- List the things for which you are grateful.
- Remind yourself of your strengths
- Journal.
- Create visual art, music, dance, or foodie art.
- Distract your mind with something you enjoy.

Ready

The final stage of the water cycle is **condensation,** where water droplets in the air come together to form clouds. Just as this cycle entails water forming new and healthy clouds, *ready* entails your healthy plan to come together, allowing you to move forward with positivity and control.

You can do this in a variety of ways, including:

- Talk to a trusted adult about what is flooding you.
- Reflect and come up with a plan for letting go and moving forward.
- Communicate your feelings to someone who may have led to them in a way that is repairing (share your feelings, do not blame, and ask if you can find a solution together).
- Think about ways you have gotten through negative feelings or emotions in the past.
- Accept these feelings, let them go, and reflect on what caused them/how to avoid them in the future.

HERE'S A QUICK SNAPSHOT OF POINTS TO REMEMBER:

Precipitation *release of water weighing clouds down*		**Release** *release negative energy weighing you down*
Collection *water slowly collects and gathers together*		**Relax** *slowly collect thoughts and gather composure*
Evaporation *water turns to vapor and travels back to the sky*		**Realign** *negative emotions turn to vapor and lighten up*
Condensation *water droplets move together to create anew*		**Ready** *move forward with positivity*

Purpose of Exercise:

- Determine a plan of action to deal with the cycle of negative thoughts or emotions in a refreshing, healthy, and helpful way.

What You Will Need:

- *My Refreshing Cycle Plans* activity pages

Directions:

1. Reflect on your general pattern of thoughts, behaviors, and actions in relation to the following negative feelings or emotions:
   - fear or worry
   - anger or frustration
   - confused or overwhelmed
   - generally negative thoughts or unidentifiable negative emotions

   (For example, when you feel fearful or worried, you may tend to shut everything out. You may isolate yourself, avoid people or situations, and you may have a hard time expressing yourself. When you feel angry or frustrated, you may lash out at those who are close to you. You may yell, throw things, and purposefully defy requests asked of you.)

2. Using the sample cycle suggestions on the previous pages, ideas from previous activities, and/or concepts of your own creation, develop a healthy and refreshing plan of action to combat these general patterns. Use the following pages to write your plans for each cycle of the corresponding negative feeling or emotion. Try to differentiate these plans to match your individual needs within each specific feeling or emotion.

3. Use these plans to guide you in moments of negative feelings and emotions. It may take a few tries to break your current patterns, but once these healthy refreshing cycles become a habit, you will notice remarkable differences in the outcome, the amount of time it takes to reach calmness, and the overall confidence you feel in your ability to overcome challenging moments.

My Refreshing Cycle Plans

1. *When I feel fearful, worried, or scared, I will:*

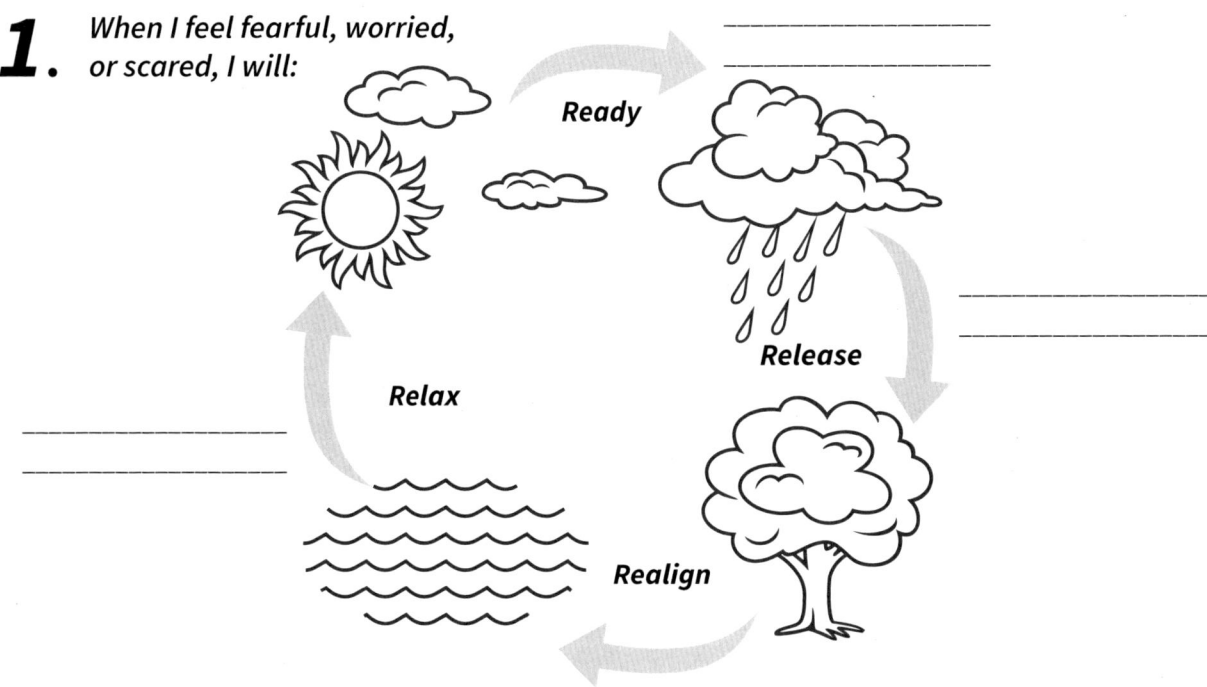

2. *When I feel angry or frustrated, I will:*

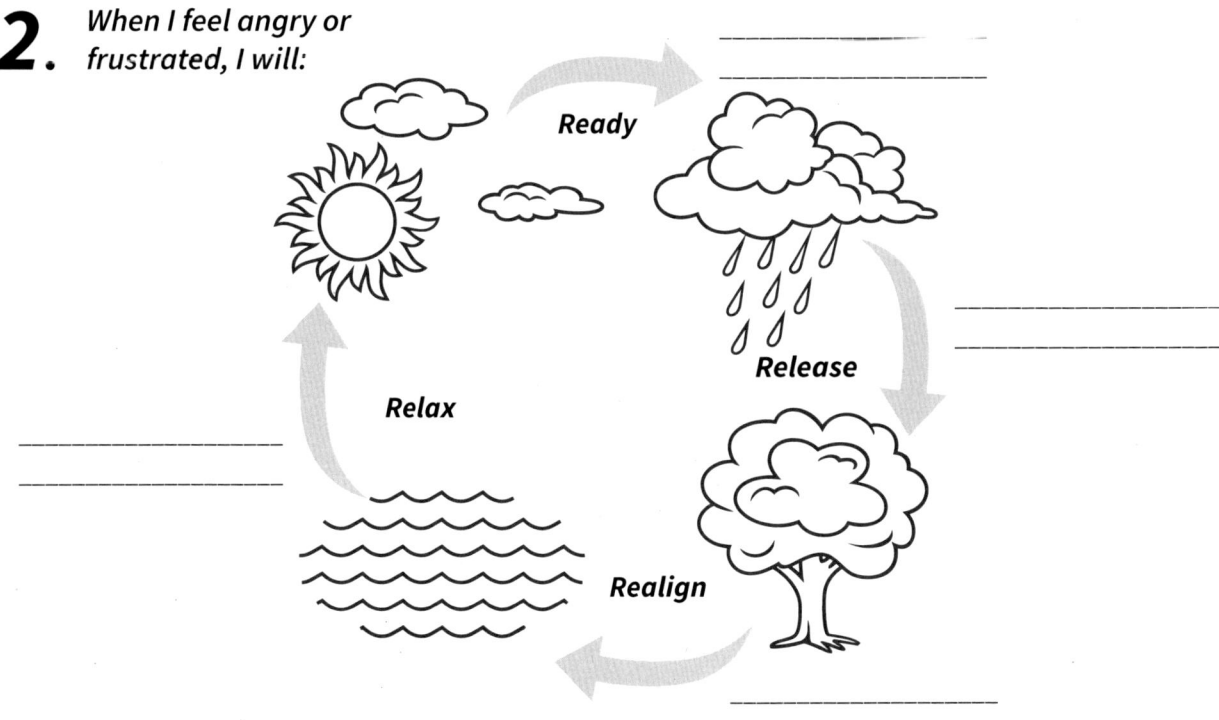

3. When I feel overwhelmed or confused, I will:

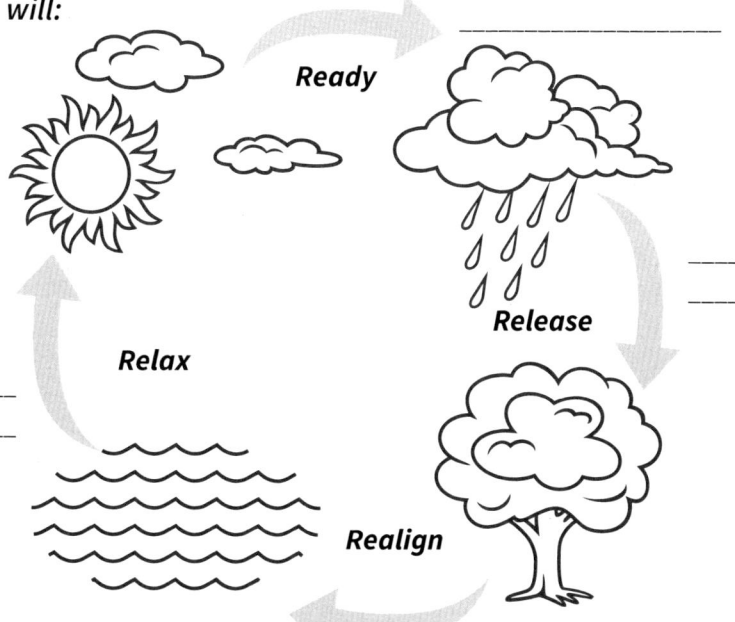

4. When I don't know what I'm feeling but need to calm down, I will:

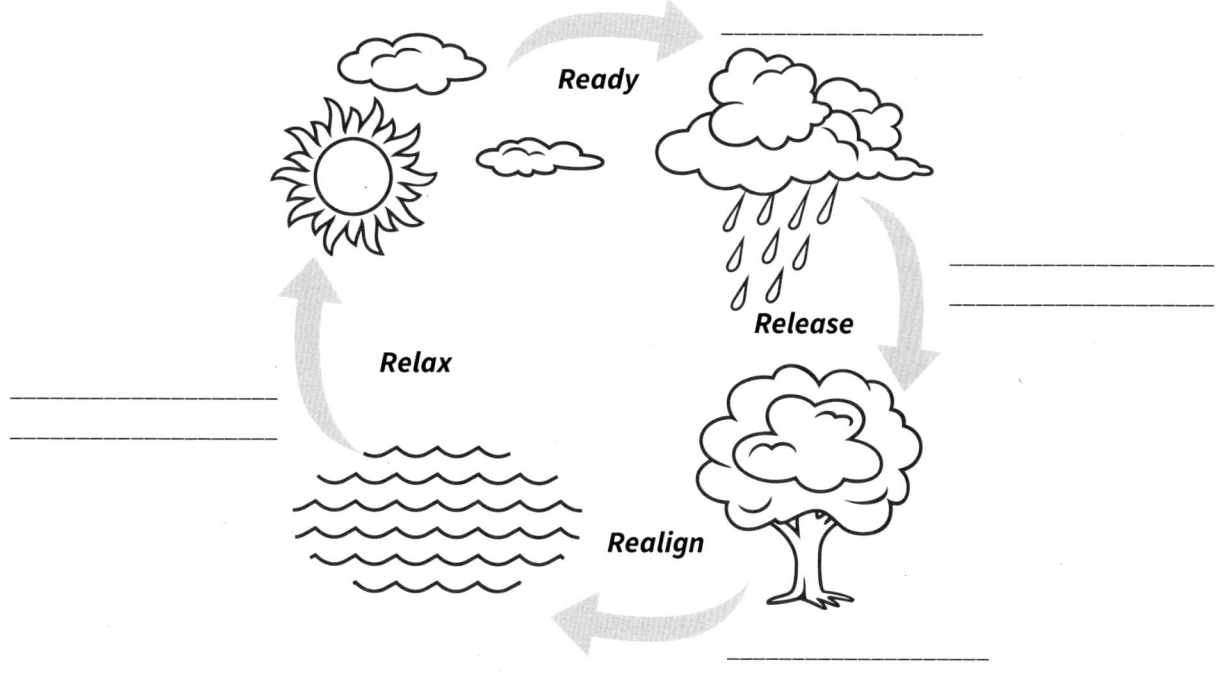

Opting for Optimism

Let's play a quick game of "Would You Rather…?" Would you rather…

1. Surround yourself with kind or unkind people?

2. Be with people who support you or people who bring you down?

3. Feel self-confidence or consistent self-doubt?

4. Enjoy most day-to-day things or find them to be frustrating?

5. Be around people who make you smile or people who make you upset?

I'll bet I know what your answer was for most of those questions. We all want joy, happiness, and positivity in our lives. The people who we surround ourselves with are a big part of whether we have the optimum amount of, well, optimism, in our lives!

Think about it… wouldn't you feel much happier overall if you were with people who made you smile, laugh, encourage you, and believe in you, as opposed to people who were always negative, only cared about themselves, or tried to make you feel like you weren't as good as them?

Negativity is contagious. When you are surrounded by negative people, it brings you down, doesn't it? It's draining and exhausting, makes you feel bad too, and is just not good for your health.

Sometimes, it's hard to recognize when you're with negative people and before you realize it, you're caught in the snowball of negativity.

Therefore, it is important to recognize the negativity that may try to creep into your life. When you recognize it, you can move away from it.

Why is this important?

Because you opt for optimism! After all, you deserve it! I know that sometimes it's hard to remind yourself of this important fact, especially when you're feeling low. But it is important that you never forget: You deserve optimism and positivity! **You deserve to be around people who recognize and respect the amazing, awesome, totally wonderful person that YOU are!**

Purpose of Exercise:

- Identify and reflect on the negative elements in your life.
- Determine how to diminish the negative and replenish the positive.

What You Will Need:

- *Opting for Optimism* short answers and drawing prompts
- *Opting for Optimism* activity page

List a few of the reasons why you deserve to be around positive and optimistic people:

_____

_____

_____

_____

Draw a picture of what you think "optimism" looks like. It can be a person, animal, thing, color, shape… whatever you'd like!

Draw a picture of what you think "negativity" looks like. It can be a person, animal, thing, color, shape… whatever you'd like!

So, how can you spot negative people? Well, they may be:
- Victims: try to make you feel guilty
- Controlling or manipulative: try to make you a puppet
- Takers: expect your time and attention but do not reciprocate
- Always right: or at least try to make you think they are, and try to make you feel like you are not as good as them
- Uncaring: especially when it comes to your feelings and boundaries

If you know anyone who fits any of these descriptions, you can opt for optimism by:
- Reminding yourself they do not own you and you are your own person who deserves to be treated with kindness and respect.
- Blocking them from your social media and choosing to be kind, but not overly friendly, when you see them.
- Choosing to ignore or disengage when they try to get you trapped in defeating or negative conversations.
- Seeking out people who make you feel good, who you enjoy, and who believe in you.

Opting for Optimism

Can you think of other ways to defeat negativity? What about ways to opt for optimism? _____
_____
_____
_____
_____
_____

Can you think of anyone who could support you in opting for optimism? _____
_____
_____
_____
_____
_____

What will the world look like when you view it from a lens of optimism (what will you focus on, care about…)? _____
_____
_____
_____
_____
_____

What will you look like to the world when people see you opting for optimism (tone, body language, facial expressions…)? _____
_____
_____
_____
_____
_____

NOTES

Immediate Reflection Notes
Confidence-Boosting, Strength, and Resilience

Congratulations! You have just completed the final section "Confidence-Boosting, Strength, and Resilience." The purpose of this section was to help you develop a positive mindset and sense of self, to increase affirming self-talk, and to strengthen your overall resiliency. While this section is fresh in your mind, take a moment to reflect on the following:

Interesting discoveries I made about myself are…

_____

_____

_____

_____

Interesting discoveries I made about strength, grit, positive thinking, and resiliency are…

_____

_____

_____

_____

I am still curious and want to learn more about…

_____

_____

_____

_____

I can strengthen my resiliency and positive thinking every day by…

_____

_____

_____

_____

I can extend these ideas into my everyday life by…

_____

_____

_____

_____

Using this new knowledge, my goals for strengthening my confidence and resiliency include (try to make no more than 3 goals)…

1 _____
_____
_____
_____

2 _____
_____
_____
_____

3 _____
_____
_____
_____

SIGNATURE _____ DATE _____
this will be useful for the check-in reflection intro

Self Check-In Reflection Notes
Confidence-Boosting, Strength, and Resilience

It has been _____ days since I have completed my reflection on "Confidence-Boosting, Strength, and Resilience." In that reflection, I set the following goals for strengthening my self-confidence and resilience:

1 _____
_____

2 _____
_____

3 _____
_____

If I were to rate myself on how I'm doing when it comes to reaching these goals, I would give myself a (on a scale of 1 to 5: 1=not close at all, 5=super successful)… ☐

A few barriers and snags I've hit along the way are… _____
_____
_____

Some things that have helped me get closer to obtaining my goals are… _____
_____
_____

To keep moving forward, I need… _____
_____

In order to reach my goals, I am committed to… _____
_____

Doodle Page

These pages are for you and you alone. Use them for your own creative self-expression. Write lyrics, make lists, draw, color, whatever your heart desires.

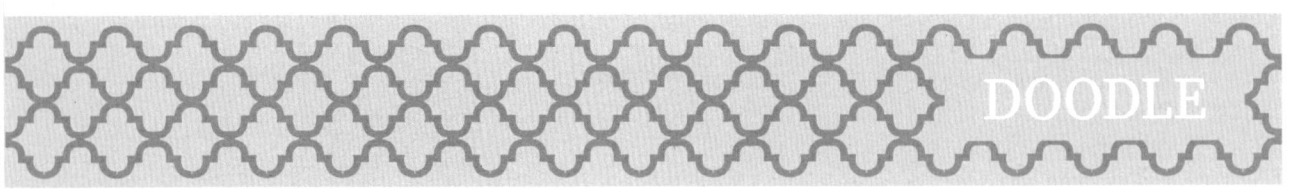

Doodle Page

These pages are for you and you alone. Use them for your own creative self-expression. Write lyrics, make lists, draw, color, whatever your heart desires.